RAISING SPIRITUAL CHAMPIONS

NURTURING YOUR CHILD'S HEART, MIND AND SOUL

GEORGE BARNA

Cover Design by Mackenna Cotten

Arizona Christian University Press
1 W Firestorm Way
Glendale, AZ 85306

Published in association with The Fedd Agency, Inc., a literary agency.

ISBN: 978-1-957616-47-6
eISBN: 978-1-957616-48-3

LCCN: 2023909393

Printed in the United States of America

TABLE OF CONTENTS

PREFACE

Two decades ago I stumbled onto what became one of the most important ministry discoveries of my life. It was an accident that changed my life—except that it was not really an accident. There are no accidents in life. Over time, it became clear that the "accidental discovery" was actually a direct and strategic message to me from God.

For about a dozen years, back when I still owned and led the Barna Research Group (which I eventually sold in 2009), one of the primary vehicles through which we disseminated our research findings was research-based ministry seminars that I led in churches in various geographic markets across the nation. My family and I were joined on those trips by Barna Group team members. In each of the more than a hundred different geographic markets we visited, we held day-long events where we had the privilege of sharing our research and commentary with an average of about 200 pastors and other ministry leaders.

We preceded each of those fourteen-month seminar tours with an eighteen-month period of research that formed the basis of the content delivered in the forthcoming seminars. We would identify four topics, do extensive national research on the topics chosen, then share the most compelling findings and implications in each of the four, ninety-minute seminar sessions offered in the markets we visited. It was an exhausting but rewarding and fruitful adventure.

As we approached what became our last seminar tour, our team met to determine the topics we would research in advance of the tour. We selected the first three topics rather quickly but struggled to identify an appropriate final topic. Having done three prior tours, we had already researched most of the hot topics in which church and ministry professionals had an interest.

We had taken on subjects such as understanding and responding to cultural trends, transformational discipleship practices, effective worship, worldview development, improving congregational stewardship, proven evangelistic strategies, visionary leadership, building Christ-centered community, generational differences, community service that changes lives, and more.

After some brainstorming and debating, we agreed upon a final topic, one that I grudgingly agreed to because it seemed to me like little more than filler. That topic was ministry to children.

During the subsequent eighteen months, as we conducted the research, and I developed the related session content, I was stunned. That "filler" topic turned out to be perhaps the most important topic we could have explored. As we discovered more and more from the ensuing research, my thinking about the importance of ministering to children shifted 180 degrees. I came to realize that if we do not get it right with young children, the chances are good that we will never see those people mature into real disciples of Jesus.

In retrospect, I can see how my initial disinterest in the topic—or I'll call it what it was: skepticism and doubt—pushed me into examining areas of ministering to children that nobody else had ventured into at that point. Dipping into divergent dimensions of childhood spiritual development certainly gave me, and hopefully others, more than a few eye-opening revelations.

The outcomes from that research became the driving message of a book called *Transforming Children into Spiritual Champions*. To my continuing surprise, that book not only became one of my bestselling books but also one of my works that has had the deepest and longest-lasting ministry impact.

But that research was developed around the start of the millennium. In the past twenty-plus years, a lot has changed. If and how we minister to children, and the context in which such ministry occurs, is quite different today than it was in 2003. Among the significant shifts are a virtually total turnover in the parenting corps; altered attitudes about Christianity, the Bible, local churches, and their children's ministries; new perspectives on parenting; changes in lifestyle fostered by the pandemic, advances in technology, and sociopolitical transitions; and continued changes in the worldview of Americans.

All these new approaches to life, updated perspectives, and the evolving role of family and faith have implications for children and how we share with them God's principles, commands, truths, and love.

STARTING WELL, FINISHING WELL

In the midst of that societal change arose two concepts that have helped to motivate and define this book.

The first is that for someone to fulfill their potential and God-given calling, it is important for them to receive a strong start in life. Entering teenage and adult years without specific types of life preparation leaves that person at a disadvantage. No one likes to start from a deficit. Life is hard enough without being handicapped from the beginning.

The ways in which we think about and engage in preparing children for life play a central role in who they become. The research is very clear that the more biblically prepared a child is to address life, the more likely they are to embrace a Christlike approach to daily challenges. Conversely, the less biblically trained a child is, the less likely it is that they will ever become a genuine disciple of Jesus Christ. The Holy Spirit can instantly transform any life at any moment, but years of data suggest that such miraculous transformations are the exception, not the norm.

Knowing this, I feel a sense of urgency to wake up people—especially the parents of young children as well as individuals who have significant cultural influence—to understand that time is of the essence in transforming how we raise children.

We can confidently predict what the future of the world will look like by carefully studying the way that children are raised today. What we invest in young lives will produce outcomes that we can foresee. If we treat children as vulnerable spiritual beings whose faith is being formed now, we will have fewer predicaments to solve in the future. The better we can instill biblical beliefs and behaviors into the minds and hearts of children, the better off we (and they) will be for decades to come.

Second, as I enter my twilight years of ministry, I am committed to finishing well. As a disciple of Jesus, that means I am devoted to optimizing my remaining time on Earth by equipping people of influence—those who are likely to exert the greatest impact on the future. With that in my mind, there is no people group to focus on that is more significant than children.

The more I can help those who work with children to create a lasting, positive impact on their lives—parents, extended family, teachers, media and technology developers, ministry practitioners, and public policy developers—the more confident I am that my final years will have brought honor to God and advanced His kingdom on Earth.

NEW RESEARCH, NEW INSIGHTS

Initiating a major project like this one has been a challenging undertaking. Before beginning the primary research for this book, I spent months and a significant amount of money seeking out knowledge and insights related to the topic at hand. Through this exploration, one thing became abundantly clear: there is no lack of information related to the spiritual development of children and the role that parents and communities of faith play in that spiritual development process.

However, it also became undeniably clear that for a focus that needs to be at the forefront of Christian activity, there is surprisingly little *objective* information about conditions and practices related to the faith, discipleship, and worldview of children. Most available content centers on opinions, emotions, individual experiences, creative ideas, anecdotes, hopes, and desires of well-intentioned authority figures. That information is not worthless, but much of it may be best taken with caution.

This book aims to fill an apparent gap in the marketplace. It is a product of a collaborative effort between the Cultural Research Center at Arizona Christian University (www.CulturalResearchCenter. com) and the Family Research Council (www.frc.org) to assist people and organizations committed to addressing the spiritual development of children in America.

Toward that end, we have conducted seven original research studies related to the ability to intentionally and strategically raise spiritual champions among the nation's children. Those national projects have focused on the following:

- Exploring the ways in which parents think about raising their children, and how faith fits into their paradigm

- Documenting the worldview foundation and spiritual perspectives of eight-to-twelve-year-olds

- Identifying the worldview and spiritual perspectives of teenagers, ages thirteen through eighteen

- Ascertaining the worldview and spiritual perspectives of the parents of children under the age of thirteen

- Determining the worldview and spiritual perspectives of Christian church-based ministers whose primary focus is children

- Analyzing content in various samples of popular child-targeted media

- Studying the ministry practices and perspectives of churches that focus on discipling children, and how worldview development fits into their outreach to children

Those research efforts were carefully developed to provide direct and pragmatic insights into the thoughts and actions of the major players who are shaping America's children.

Analyzed as a whole, these projects provide us with unique insights into what Americans believe about children and what they are experiencing; the role of faith and spirituality in the lives of children; the preparation and commitment of Christian churches to helping prepare parents in the faith formation of their children; what parents are thinking and doing regarding the formulation of their children's faith experience and perspectives; and what the popular media and technology are doing to influence the lives of our young people.

In other words, this book is an outgrowth of several core principles I have held and taught for decades:

- Making good decisions requires good information; the more objective and problem-specific data you have and use, the less likely you are to make bad decisions.

- To be effective, invest most of your resources where they can make the biggest difference.

- Never assume that what worked in the past will work in the present.

- A practice that is popular or common is not necessarily useful or effective.

- Anecdotes are interesting, but data are helpful and reliable.

- You get what you measure.

Although it is my name on the book, this work is more than one man's commitment to serving God by studying the spirituality of America's children and those who influence them. This is a collaborative work involving the thoughts and efforts of people from Arizona Christian University, Family Research Council, various churches, teachers, administrators at Christian schools, and numerous parents. I believe it is fair to say that we share a common desire: advancing the kingdom of God by wisely and lovingly equipping children to engage with God.

Our joint prayer is that the insights in these pages will motivate influencers to elevate the truth of His words and teachings in the minds, hearts, and souls of the nation's youngest people, and facilitate the emergence of multiple generations of spiritual champions.

Our national refusal or failure to do so will almost certainly bring the Christian Church in the United States to collapse, if not near extinction, with all the related cultural ramifications of such a calamity.

Simply put, we are called by God to raise children to become spiritual champions—youngsters who mature into transformed and transformational followers of Jesus Christ. We can do this!

To get off to a good start in that quest, we must make a firm commitment and gain practical insights into how to best fulfill the commitment. I believe the information in this book will help us do so.

–GEORGE BARNA

Professor, Arizona Christian University
Director of Research, Cultural Research Center at Arizona Christian University
Senior Research Fellow, Center for Biblical Worldview, Family Research Council
April 2023

SECTION ONE
THE IMPORTANCE OF CHILDREN

This book has three sections. This first section contains three chapters. The first of those describes the importance of children and the opportunity to disciple them. The second chapter addresses how well existing ministry to children is faring. The third chapter is based on research insights about our efforts to fulfill the Great Commission and considers why we should be energetically focused on making disciples of children.

The second section of the book details what it takes to make a disciple, digging into the four practices that characterize genuine disciples of Jesus.

The third and final section focuses on how media and church-based ministries are impacting the lives of children. This section includes a discussion of how parents and other influencers can interact with media and churches most effectively in the campaign to disciple children.

01
MAKING THE MOST OF YOUR LIFE

n recent years, large and increasing numbers of Americans have been struggling with the purpose, meaning, direction, value, and joy in their life. Statistics from national studies by the Cultural Research Center at Arizona Christian University show that two out of every three adults under the age of forty (67%) say they are still trying to identify the meaning and purpose of their life.

A mere 22% believe that life itself is sacred, which helps to explain why suicide rates have skyrocketed and abortion remains a popular option to an unplanned pregnancy. Further, most young adults (54%) admit that they often feel anxious, depressed, or unsafe.[1]

It is not only individuals who are struggling with life; our society as a whole is frustrated with the way things are going too. Three out of four adults are angry about conditions in America. About two-thirds of adults agree that the country is headed in the wrong direction.[2] Fewer than three out of every ten adults are very satisfied with their life today. And less than two out of five adults are very satisfied with the nation's moral conditions, quality of parenting, the viewpoints taught in the public schools, or the quality of life for our children.[3]

Perhaps that sense of disappointment is what motivates a large majority of Americans to take actions intended to turn things around. If you look closely, you'll see that a gigantic share of Americans engage in behaviors they hope will change the world for the better. More than nine out of ten donate some of their resources (i.e., money or time) for that purpose.[4] Two out of three adults contact elected officials to thank them for courageous or appropriate action, or to exhort them to take such initiative.[5] The growth in the number of people who care enough to boycott brands, products, or companies whose choices conflict with the perceived best interests of the country has increased significantly in the past twenty years. A majority of our fellow citizens—even some of the irreligious ones—regularly pray for the needs and positive outcomes of others.[6] Recent government statistics indicate that most Americans—more than 170 million—have signed up to be organ donors to assist those in need.[7]

What does that information tell us? Clearly, we want our life to matter. We want to make a difference in the world, a chance to have a positive impact. In fact, almost everyone—96% according to one recent survey—believes their actions can make a difference in the world.[8]

My own research has shown that having a positive influence on the world is one of the life goals of more than three out of four adults. In addition, about three-fourths of us (72%) believe that meaning in life comes from contributing value to the world in which we live.[9]

Most Americans don't just want to take up space on the planet, they want to impact it. Most of us don't possess a victim mentality. We believe we can make things better, and through that impact our lives count for something meaningful. You are probably one of these people.

But possessing the desire to make a difference is not enough. The mere desire begs the question: How? What can you do to ensure that you improve lives in a tangible way?

HOW TO MAKE A DIFFERENCE

Your chief purpose in life—and the pathway to joy, fulfillment, meaning, and flourishing—is to know, love, and serve God with all your heart, soul, mind, and strength. Jesus said so (Mark 12:29–30). So your challenge is to understand who He made you to be, the circumstances in which He has placed you, the abilities and resources He has given to you, and how you can apply those resources and abilities within your circumstances to honor Him.

Jesus gave us direct clues as to what making a difference means. At the end of His life on Earth, He exhorted His followers to do three related tasks: Make disciples of all the nations, baptize those disciples, and teach them to obey God's commands.[10]

Earlier in His ministry, Jesus described what qualified someone to be a disciple. As He taught His own disciples, He initially declared that someone is His disciple if they obey His teaching. A short time later, He added that a disciple is someone who loves the other followers of Christ. And He later rounded out the discussion by noting that a genuine disciple also produces substantial spiritual fruit. In another setting, He instructed His followers that someone could not be His disciple unless they always placed God first in their life, surrendered everything to follow Him, and completely submitted to His authority.[11]

The ultimate means to making a difference in this world, then, is for you to make disciples—that is, to live wholeheartedly and boldly for God, equip people to obey His teachings, love other believers, and produce spiritual fruit. But to *make* a disciple, you must first *be* a disciple.

So we quickly arrive at a fairly simple description of what our life is to look like: a disciple who makes disciples. This is the proverbial win-win situation. Your life is optimized by being a disciple. And by reproducing your love and devotion to Christ, you help to positively transform the lives of others. In doing so, you bring joy and glory to your Father in Heaven. Who loses out in this commitment to discipleship? Only Satan.

MAKING DISCIPLES

To succeed at disciple-making, though, requires a thoughtful and diligent commitment to the process. Turning again to the research, what have we learned in recent years about effective disciple-making?

First, nobody can be forced into being a disciple. It is an act of will by each individual. As a disciple-maker, then, you must realize that "making disciples" is beyond your capacity. The best you can hope to do is become a disciple and then appropriate the power and wisdom of the Holy Spirit to encourage others to choose to become disciples. With that choice in place, you may then follow the pathway that is most likely to lead them to genuine discipleship.

Second, making adults into disciples is extraordinarily difficult. The primary reason is that their worldview has already been established and, according to the research, changes very little, if at all, after the age of thirteen. That's right, *by the age of thirteen, most people's worldview is so deeply formed that it rarely endures significant change.*

This leads to one of the most important facts for you to absorb: *A person's worldview starts developing in the fifteen-month to eighteen-month age range and is largely in place by the age of thirteen. That's the prime window of opportunity for discipleship.* If a person is not inclined to buy into the claims of Christ and the practices He preached by the time they reach high school, the chances of them ever doing so are slim, and the probability gets slimmer with each passing year they are alive.

The Holy Spirit can change any person, at any time, in the blink of an eye—but, on average, such bold change does not happen among teens and adults. If a biblical worldview foundation is not in place by a person's thirteenth birthday, they are highly unlikely to become a devoted and passionate follower of Jesus Christ before they die.

This is underscored by the fact that about two-thirds of all Americans who ever accept Jesus Christ as their Savior do so before the age of thirteen. (We will discuss these matters more extensively in the next two chapters.)

But why, you might ask, is having a biblical worldview such a big deal? Can't you become a committed disciple of the Lord by regularly attending church services and reading the Bible, by donating money to a church or other ministries, and being part of a small group? In fact, isn't that the practical, functional definition of a disciple? That's certainly what most churches believe, teach, and model. Is it wrong?

Sadly, that *is* an erroneous conception of discipleship. Settling for immersion in the religious game is one of the very things that Jesus died to eliminate, as evidenced by His rocky relationship with the religious leaders of His day, especially the Pharisees.

Remember the behaviors He enumerated as the marks of a disciple? Love God more than anyone else. Abandon anything that hinders your love of God or ability to follow Him. Accept His authority over all aspects of your life. Obey His teaching. Love other people. Produce spiritual fruit. Envision the lifestyle that such a commitment produces. When consistently and joyfully practiced, that lifestyle motivates other people to become enthusiastic, fully engaged disciples.

Spend some time reflecting on what He said—and did *not* say. For instance,

- Jesus *did not* command people to attend church services regularly. He did call for His followers to meet together and to worship God in the company of other believers. But the way He modeled that with His disciples was typically through shared meals and experiences, by intensely discussing the meaning and application of the Scriptures, and by serving other people. He seemed greatly unimpressed by religiosity—that is, routinely attending religious events and deploying rote religious practices.

- Jesus *did not* say that your spiritual development is the responsibility of, nor is it determined by, religious leaders or organizations (such as pastors or local churches). He pushed His disciples to take responsibility for their own righteousness and lifestyle choices. He taught them to lean on the power and guidance of God rather than the input and regulations championed by religious officials and organizations.

- Jesus *did not* teach that discipleship is about emotional connection to an ideology, movement, or persona. His conception of Christianity was deeply rooted in understanding God—His nature, purposes, truth principles, standards, and promises—and applying that understanding to produce a biblically consistent lifestyle that revolves around God rather than self. The Bible's concept of love is not about generating warm, fuzzy feelings regarding other people; it is about grace-based acceptance of others, just as Christ sacrificed Himself for all creation.

Why does that matter? Because these kinds of insights shape an understanding of life—a worldview—that should influence every decision we make. That is what a biblical worldview does: It judges every option you face in light of scriptural truths and commands.

If a disciple is a person transformed by the love of Christ to become like Christ, the means to that end is through their worldview—the intellectual, emotional, and spiritual filter you apply to every situation so that your choices and decisions reflect the ways of the Lord. (We will dig more deeply into worldview development and application in chapters 5 and 6.)

The bottom line, then, is that if you want your life to make an impact, you must be committed to being a disciple who makes disciples. And the research clearly indicates that the most effective approach to disciple-making is to focus on discipling children. To effectively disciple a child entails developing their worldview to be consistent with the Lord's teachings.

Raising children to be spiritual champions—that is, followers of Jesus Christ—is the only real hope for any nation, family, or individual. It is during a person's first dozen years on Earth that they amass the knowledge, relationships, experiences, and wisdom that shape their lifelong perspectives on how the world works, their place in that world, and how they will carry out their vision of self and life for the duration of their stay on the planet.

THE GRAND CALLING

Let me propose to you that each of us who loves God and is committed to living for His purposes has a shared "grand calling." This grand calling is comprised of four fundamental expectations that God has of those who are disciples. In fact, those four components of the grand calling point us toward making disciples.

Take a deeper look at this quartet of holy pursuits.

THE GREAT COMMISSION

Most Christians are familiar with the passage of Scripture known as the Great Commission. Jesus entreated us in Matthew 28:19 to "go, make disciples of all the nations." Oddly, this portion of Scripture is often misinterpreted as a call for evangelism; in reality, it is a command regarding disciple-making.

A related point of confusion is the widespread belief that when someone becomes "born again"—that is, when they recognize their sinfulness, confess their sins to God, and ask Him to spare them their rightful eternal punishment because of the atoning death of Jesus Christ—their discipleship journey has been completed. On the contrary, becoming born again is just one step in the aggregate, lifelong process of becoming a new creation in Christ.

The Great Commission is our basic call to action as disciples. As the final words of Christ to His followers, He was reiterating the most important task He had assigned to them—and to us. It is not simply a call to evangelize, although that is part of the mission. The end game is to lead people to dedicate themselves to following Jesus as the Lord of their life, beyond simply claiming Him as their Savior.

Those who recite the "prayer of salvation" and believe they have guaranteed themselves eternal security without experiencing a life-transforming change of heart and lifestyle are guilty of what Dietrich Bonhoeffer calls "cheap grace."[12] That is the act of assuming that God's grace to sinners is not only free but costless, i.e., cheap. Cheap grace is nothing more than a comfortable but illegitimate facsimile of the true grace of Jesus experienced by those who are genuinely repentant and surrendered to God.[13]

Producing spiritual fruit requires a commitment to experiencing a new life in Christ by pursuing the ways and purposes He outlined for us.

THE GREAT COMMANDMENT

Embracing what Jesus described as "the most important commandment" is a challenge that is widely recognized among believers. In this exhortation, Jesus explained, "The Lord our God is the one and only

Lord. And you must love the Lord your God with all your heart, all your soul, all your mind, and all your strength."[14]

President Donald Trump gained notoriety for advancing what is known as his "America first" doctrine. Jesus is even more famous for His own proclamation that we must live with a "God first" mentality. The connection of this way of thinking to the Great Commission is important. We tangibly express our love for God by acknowledging and energetically doing His expressed will, which is to make disciples.

Making disciples reflects our own commitment to serving Him because we would not bother if we were not fully sold-out to Him. Fulfilling the Great Commission reflects our love for Him. And our engagement in sharing the ways of God with other disciples is a means by which we share our knowledge of who He is.

THE GREAT COMMITMENT

The Great Commission and the Great Commandment are God's exhortations to us. The "Great Commitment" is our response to those exhortations. Why do we need to consider the depth of our response? Because simply agreeing with the "rightness" of the concepts Jesus proclaimed is not enough to make anyone a disciple, much less a disciple-maker.

When you fully cooperate with God to bring about your life transformation, you move beyond assenting to precepts and into inviting Him to transform you into the person He created and desires you to be. The Great Commitment is about agreeing with the Great

Commission and Great Commandment so profoundly that you rebuild your life around them—and the evidence of that commitment is irrefutably available for all to see and experience.

The Great Commitment is your promise to God that you will apply yourself to carrying out those challenges—with His authority, in His power, and for His glory. And make no mistake about it, living like Christ and leading people to Christ and then building them up in the Christian life is an intense commitment.

When it comes to making disciples, a close examination of faith in the American context reveals the need to strategically shift our focus from prioritizing ministry to adults to investing in reaching and influencing children. It is not that adults (including yourself) are unimportant or of lesser value to God; all human lives are sacred, and every person matters to God. If you encounter an opportunity to disciple an adult, do it! God does not discriminate on the basis of age, and neither should we. But as you ponder how to serve the Lord by making disciples, recognize that the greatest return on the investment of your ministry resources, with the longest-lasting effect, is achieved by spiritually discipling children.

As we will explore in subsequent chapters, children spend the first twelve years of their life filling a spiritual vacuum. They have numerous choices, and their spiritual development will be challenged on a regular basis by the information and experiences they encounter every day. By the time a person reaches their teenage years, they have typically drawn personal conclusions about the most important spiritual matters. Those conclusions can be altered, but my research shows that such alterations are the exception to the norm. Adults are even less likely than teenagers to jump from their existing spiritual perspectives to different points of view. Childhood is when critical decisions are made about every dimension of life, including the spiritual.

Anyone who is determined to love God by making disciples is best positioned to do so by targeting children. There is nothing wrong with targeting other population groups, but we ought not to lean toward those alternative people groups by default or out of personal comfort. Our ministry strategy, including which segments we will target, must be intentional and strategic.

If you are tempted to write off this challenge as irrelevant to you, let me also note that the research shows an overwhelming majority of Americans have some relationships or regular interaction with children.

If you are a parent, then discipling your child(ren) is your primary responsibility in life.[15] (Really!) If you are a grandparent, you have a tremendous opportunity to influence your grandkids. Maybe you own or work in a retail business, in which case you may encounter children continually. Perhaps you love sports and could exert spiritual influence by being a volunteer coach or assistant coach. The engagement options are too numerous to list here. The point is that very few Americans can truthfully claim they have no opportunities to relate to and potentially disciple children.

Consider also the fact that as a disciple of Christ, God has provided you with special abilities—spiritual gifts—that will empower you as a disciple-maker. In Romans 12:6–13 and 1 Corinthians 12:1–11, Paul writes about these special abilities. While their deployment is not to be limited to working with children, or limited to making disciples, the act of raising children to be spiritual champions would be a valuable application of your gifts.

Your life is filled with opportunities to do interesting or important things—in fact, you have so many options that you may become distracted from what matters the most. As you think about how you will spend your time and other resources, make it a point to prioritize disciple-making. Indeed, it is a matter of commitment.

THE GREAT CONSIGNMENT

Time is relentless. It moves forward at the same pace regardless of cultural or personal conditions and efforts. Inevitably, power and authority will pass from those who have it now to those who are being groomed for it in the future. That reality is every bit as true for communities of faith as it is for other groups of people (political parties, corporations, schools, etc.). The children we raise today will be the leaders of the future church. Whether they will be ready for those responsibilities or not, we will eventually consign faith leadership to the children of our society.

Children, then, are not just your primary personal legacy; they represent your eternal legacy as well. How well you disciple them now will determine the direction, strength, and impact of the body of Christ in America for decades to come. Your children, or children whom you influence, are your spiritual heirs. They will shepherd the church at large through the challenges that emerge based on how well you disciple them.

As you ponder these interlinked aspects of your divine calling—the Great Commission, Great Commandment, Great Commitment, and Great Consignment—a sense of your role in forming the future arises. It is a portrait still being created—and, therefore, one that you may still mold through the human clay you help to sculpt.

The more immersed you become in owning the role of disciple-maker—someone who attractively and consistently models devotion to God by equipping children to participate in the unfolding of His truth and its impact—the more clear and joyful your efforts will be.

A SPECIAL WORD TO PARENTS

One of the realities the Bible makes clear is that children are special to God—and so is the role of a parent. We have an abundance of Bible passages—literally dozens of verses, stories, principles, and commands—about children and parents who convey God's perspectives. It would be fruitful to read through those to grasp God's point of view, and to consider how they relate to your own thoughts and actions. Let me summarize some of those ideas.

CHILDREN MATTER TO GOD

God seems to take special pleasure in the nature of children, and He wants you to experience that same joy. He entreats men and women to get married and have children, raising them in a loving and nurturing environment.

It is clear that God is not interested in watching children grow up from afar; He wants a genuine relationship with children. Toward that end, He explains how children may enter His presence and enjoy Him, just as He enjoys their nature and unique personalities.

Jesus demonstrated His love of young people by not only personally blessing children but also by issuing a warning against doing anything that would harm them.[16]

RAISING CHILDREN IS PRIMARILY THE FAMILY'S JOB

Children have a special place in God's heart, and He entrusts them to parents as a gift—something special that He shares with us as a sign of His love for us and the value of life itself. He expects children to become a conduit of personal fulfillment and special blessings to their parents.

But with the blessing of children comes responsibility. Children arrive as clay to be molded and refined, particularly in how they think about God and His expectations and how they relate to Him. This means parents are responsible for teaching their children about God and His ways and for disciplining them to think and act in a manner that reflects the life of Christ. Parents have primary responsibility for the total well-being of their children—education, discipline, protection—but the most vital aspect of their development is spiritual formation.

Their spiritual development takes various forms: being baptized into the faith, studying the Bible, obeying His commands, living in resonance with His life principles, asking for forgiveness, practicing spiritual acts and disciplines (such as worship and prayer) that honor Him, and advancing His kingdom on Earth.

To raise spiritual champions, parents must disciple their children. Such firmness of leadership is most effective when accomplished through mutual trust and sharing. The Scriptures assert that the parent-child relationship will greatly benefit from parents' modeling the lessons they convey.[17]

What matters to God must matter to you. Children are of paramount importance to Him and must be of similar importance to you. You prove that shared interest not only through talk but by your actions. If you are dedicated to following scriptural advice about how to raise your children, seeking to develop them as spiritual champions more than anything else, then you are doing God's work and bringing Him joy. Raising Christlike children is the ultimate legacy.

MOVING FORWARD

It has been said Jesus did not die for a cause or a movement; He died for people. He did that because He loves us and wants us to live our best life, according to His standards and expectations.

Living that kind of life in which you imitate the life of Christ is a serious commitment. It is not simply about your personal experiences on Earth but also about how you affect the lives of others—especially children. When God reviews your life after you leave Earth, how well you connected with and influenced the lives of children will be on the agenda.

He definitely placed you here, at this time in history, to make a difference in the lives of other people. He has not asked you to save the world—Jesus has already accomplished that—but He has called you to be an agent of transformation, and there is no better way to fulfill that calling than to focus on discipling children.

Are you willing to commit yourself wholeheartedly to that assignment?

02

REALIGNING OUR COURSE TRAJECTORY

n the first chapter, we considered the fact that most people—probably including you—want their life to make a difference. Then we turned to the Bible and concluded that the optimum way to make a difference is by making disciples of Jesus Christ. And we discovered that the most effective way to make disciples is to invest in the lives of children, raising them to be spiritual champions.

But what does it mean to be a spiritual champion? One way of describing a spiritual champion is someone who is devoted to fully imitating the life of Christ—thinking like Him, acting like Him, and living for Him.

With that profile in mind, we can determine how well we are doing at producing spiritual champions. If we are achieving satisfactory results, we should identify what we did to develop such individuals and continue to replicate those actions. But if we are falling short of the mark, our challenge is to figure out why, and then determine what we can do to implement a better disciple-making model.

Let's agree that your goal is to be a responsible parent, and that a responsible parent is one who raises spiritual champions.[18] Period. With that in mind, we need to determine whether the steps taken by parents are producing the desired end product—disciples of Jesus. To do so, we can evaluate the beliefs and behaviors of post-adolescents, focusing on thirteen- and fourteen-year-olds as the immediate product of our attempts at equipping children to grow into Christ's disciples while they are in their primary stage of spiritual formation.

EVIDENCE OF THE DISCIPLED CHILDREN

Because a person's preparation for following Christ is typically in place by the age of thirteen, we can fairly accurately predict the future of the church by assessing how well the discipleship process has fared among young people by the time they reach the end of that spiritually fertile period (i.e., what has happened in their life through age twelve).

Surveying the population of thirteen- and fourteen-year-olds will give us a good grip on how well we have done over the past decade of discipling and what we can expect in the years to come because of those efforts.

Right off the bat, though, our research among young teens indicates that there are some serious deficiencies that will have dramatic implications.

To start with, barely one-third of newly minted teens (36%) believe that God exists and is the all-knowing, all-powerful Creator of the universe, who is perfect and just, and who rules the universe today. In contrast, closer to half (43%) are *Don'ts*—people who don't know if there is a God, don't believe in His existence, or don't care one way or the other.[19]

At the same time, we find severe deficits in their knowledge of the character of Jesus. A majority of the youngest teens (61%) either believe Jesus Christ sinned while He was on Earth or hold open the possibility that He did. While they have heard that He was sinless and pure, most of them are not buying it.

Things are no better when it comes to beliefs about God's adversary. Seven out of ten young teens (70%) either reject the existence of Satan or don't know if he exists. This is a major shift from the beliefs of their parents, who may not have given much thought to Satan's existence, but at least a majority of them believe Satan is real. That point-of-view has not been handed down from one generation to the next.[20]

The shakiness of the belief system of young teens is demonstrated by their thoughts about creation. Not even half of them (45%) believe that God created the universe. Even a smaller share of them—only one-third (31%)—accept the teaching that the universe and everything in it was designed, created, and is sustained by God.

One of the major weaknesses of the early-teen worldview is the prevalent perspective on truth. Only one out of every ten (10%) rejects the idea that moral truth is always relative to the individual and their circumstances. Instead, a large share believes that there are no absolute moral truths that are impervious to conditions and personal preferences. Among the many consequences of that point of view is the dismissal of the idea of sin, the rejection of the notion that Jesus Christ is the only means to eternal salvation, the repudiation of the Bible as a source of inerrant truth principles for everyone, and the denial that morality is predictable and consistent.

Sure enough, young teens follow through on their dismissal of the existence of absolute moral truth by expanding their war on God's ways. Just one in four (27%) identify God as the basis of all truth, as revealed in the Bible. Less than one out of every five young teens (18%) define God and His perspectives, as described in the Bible, as their most likely source of guidance when making decisions about what is right and what is wrong. Given these findings, it is disappointing but not surprising to discover that less than one out of three early teens (31%) believes that the Bible is the true and reliable words of God.

Naturally, if there is no such thing as absolute moral truth, it's difficult, if not impossible, to argue that sin exists. Most early teens don't even try. Just one out of every six (17%) agrees that people are born into sin and can only be saved from the consequences of sin by the forgiveness available through Jesus Christ. That helps to explain why a mere one out of every five (21%) believes that they will live with God in eternity after having confessed their sins and accepted Jesus Christ as their Savior. (For context, realize that this 21% who are "born-again" is just half the national average of born-agains existing among people who are fifty or older—42%.)[21] In fact, nearly twice as many believe that reincarnation is a real possibility for themselves as believe they will experience eternity in the presence of God due to their confession of sin and the grace of God provided through the death and resurrection of Jesus Christ.

These outcomes are consistent with the early-teen view that people are basically good, a belief supported by a majority of them. Neither do these young people believe that Satan is involved in the evil that happens on Earth. Only one out of every eight early teens (13%)

attribute the pain and suffering that people experience as the influence of Satan on human beings to commit sins.

Life is seen through a very different lens by early-teens than, for instance, a typical Christian who has a biblical worldview. Just one in four early-teens (26%) sees the purpose of their life as knowing, loving, and serving God with all their heart, mind, strength, and soul. Even fewer of them (17%) accept the idea that the best way to define success on Earth is by consistently obeying God.

People's lifestyle puts their belief systems on public display. Remember, you do what you believe, so your moment-to-moment activity is the best indicator of what you truly believe. We can predict the kind of society coming down the road by noting that less than three out of ten early-teens (28%) believe that God's plan for humanity is based upon families, that He considers family to be the marriage of one man to one woman, and that any other configuration for marriage or sexual intimacy is sinful, regardless of one's culture.

Another window into the mind and hearts of young people is how few of them (8%) believe that the wealth an individual accumulates is provided to them by God to manage for the advancement of His kingdom on Earth. They are far more likely to believe that they have earned what they possess and are free to use that wealth as they see fit without regard to spiritual principles or God's expectations.

Perhaps what makes some of this confusing for adults are the oft-cited claims of young people regarding their spirituality. For instance, half of early-teens (49%) describe themselves as Christians—

despite a large share of those same individuals rejecting the divinity and holiness of Christ, the authority of Scripture, and the presence and effects of sin. Our studies over the past few years have found that millions of Christians embrace the label "Christian" not because they love Jesus or accept the Bible, but because in their minds, that term implies they are basically good people.

Millennials (defined in our research as people born between 1984 and 2002, and who constitute the largest segment of parents overseeing early-teens) actively pursued alternative forms of faith and spirituality and are widely documented as having embraced the label of "spiritual but not religious."

Therefore, this younger crowd raised by them is less inclined to regularly participate in or adopt any form of traditional or popular faith. That is perhaps most evident in their religious activity. Less than one out of five of them claim to pray to God (18%), know and do God's will (19%), read or study the Bible (12%), or acknowledge their sins and seek God's forgiveness (11%) during a typical week. Just one out of five (20%) intentionally thanks, praises, or worships God during a typical week.

SUMMARIZING WHAT RECENT CHILDREN HAVE DECIDED

We just covered a lot of ground quickly. Let's summarize what our thirteen- and fourteen-year-old children have embraced as their theological foundation, one that will likely define them for the rest of their lives.

WHAT THEY BELIEVE

- 8% believe that the wealth an individual accumulates is provided to them by God for them to manage to advance His kingdom on Earth.

- 10% reject the idea that moral truth is always relative to the individual and their circumstances because there are moral absolutes.

- 13% believe the pain and suffering that people experience is due to Satan's influence.

- 17% agree that people are born into sin and can only be saved from the consequences of sin by Jesus Christ.

- 17% agree the best way to define success on Earth is consistent obedience to God.

- 18% list the Bible as their primary source of moral guidance.

- 21% believe they will live with God in eternity because they confessed their sins and accepted Jesus Christ as their Savior.

- 26% see the purpose of their life as knowing, loving, and serving God with all their heart, soul, mind, and strength.

- 27% believe that God is the basis of all truth, as revealed in the Bible.

- 28% believe that God's plan for humanity is based upon families, that He considers family to be based on the marriage of one man to one woman, and that any other configuration for marriage or sexual intimacy is sinful, regardless of one's culture.

- 31% contend that the Bible is the true and reliable words of God.

- 31% say the universe and everything in it has been designed, created, and sustained by God.

- 35% reject the notion that people are basically good.

- 36% believe that God is the omnipotent, omniscient, perfect, and just Creator of the universe who still rules it today.

- 39% believe reincarnation is a real possibility for them.

- 43% don't know if there is a God, don't believe in His existence, or don't care.

- 45% believe God created the universe.

- 49% describe themselves as Christians.

- 56% say moral truth is up to each individual; there are no moral absolutes that apply to everyone, all the time.

- 56% claim to be deeply committed to their spiritual life.

- 61% either believe Jesus Christ sinned or may have sinned while He was on Earth.

- 70% say Satan does not exist, or they don't know if he exists.

WHAT THEY DO IN A TYPICAL WEEK

- 11% acknowledge their sins and seek God's forgiveness.

- 12% read or study the Bible other than times when they are at a church event.

- 18% pray to God.

- 19% seek to know and do God's will.

- 20% intentionally thank, praise, or worship God apart from church events.

This profile helps to explain why less than 1% of thirteen- and fourteen-year-old Americans have a biblical worldview. This is a profile of a class of people immersed in spiritual turbulence and deceit. It is not a profile of spiritual champions—although, with commitment and considerable hard work, that can be turned around.

DOING WHAT WORKS IN DISCIPLE-MAKING

Previous research in which I've been involved demonstrated that parents who raised spiritual champions engaged in many similar approaches as they nurtured their children.[22] Among those shared tactics were these:

- Investing in and nurturing a solid, lasting relationship with the child

- Prioritizing spiritual development

- Establishing God, through the Bible, as the ultimate authority

- Establishing inflexible Bible-based priorities and boundaries

- Setting high but reasonable standards and expectations for them

- Inculcating traditional values and character traits

- Discipling each child with consistency of belief and behavior

- Acknowledging and working with the unique qualities and abilities of each child

- Developing structure, goals, and plans, evaluating progress, and revising accordingly

- Influencing the choice of their child's friends

- Aggressive management of the child's media exposure

- Pursuing spiritual growth concurrent with the child

- Modeling and expecting engagement in spiritual practices every day, throughout the day

- Seeking and accepting spiritual support from their faith community

One of the most important conclusions to emerge from that research was that consistency in the philosophy and practices of parents has a huge and lasting impact on children for the rest of their lives.

Know what you believe and do not depart from it. Be prepared to discuss what you believe, why you believe it, and how you try to integrate those beliefs into your lifestyle. If your child asks a question that stumps you, do not bluff your way through the exchange in order to save face. Show them how you will figure out God's way related to the situation. If your child correctly identifies a bad decision you made, based on biblical principles, acknowledge the blunder and demonstrate how to handle it. Have a plan for what you want to achieve with your child, and stick to the plan. Implementing the plan through the dozen-plus strategies and tactics identified above is invaluable.

Sadly, most parents who are born-again Christians do not utilize these practices today. Our most recent national survey of parents examined what they report to be their priorities and their most important parenting tactics. They do not offer a lot of hope for great outcomes.

- Consistency was described by the parents of now-adult spiritual champions as well as those grown children themselves as the single, most important attribute in the spiritual formation practices of those Christ followers. They uniformly emphasized the significance of having clear biblical principles as the discipling foundation, practicing those beliefs through behavior, and never deviating from the principles. Unfortunately, that wisdom has not gotten around to other parents. Our most recent study among the current class of parents who are born-again Christians found that less than half of them (45%) deem consistency to be very important in their child-raising efforts.

- Screening their child's peers to facilitate positive, high-quality relationships was a critical attribute in the eyes of parents who successfully raised spiritual champions. Yet less than half of today's born-again parents (45%) concur with the importance of that activity.

- Despite a preponderance of evidence that media exerts an enormous, lasting influence on the lives of young people, barely half of today's born-again parents (56%) consider supervising the media and technology exposure of their children to be very important. In contrast, this was listed as a necessity by parents who raised spiritual champions.

- One of the crucial practices of disciples is serving other people. Again, a minority of the current crop of born-again parents (44%) characterized this practice as very important to the way they are raising their children.

- Introducing their children to the spiritual beliefs and practices the parents personally embrace was considered a very important part of their parenting responsibility by less than three out of every five born-again parents (58%). This is a telling statistic about the unwillingness of too many born-again Christians to share their core beliefs with their own children. It suggests that religious beliefs are typically ignored by many of today's Christian parents as being central to who their children become or to their likelihood of becoming genuine disciples of Jesus.

- Requiring the active participation of their children in the life of their church body or religious community was labeled "very important" by just four out of ten born-again parents (41%).

- As noted throughout this book, intentionally shaping the worldview or philosophy of life of their child is a non-negotiable for raising a devoted follower of Christ. Because every decision the child makes for the remainder of their life is made through that filter, worldview is arguably the most important foundation a parent can help to develop. Regardless, only one out of every three born-again parents (35%) believe this practice is very important.

- There were a variety of parenting practices that today's parents credited with being more important than shaping their child's worldview. Among those were helping them to excel in academics, ensuring their childhood is fun and carefree, frequently discussing the child's life experiences, and facilitating exercise and excellent physical health.

Effective parenting is not a pick-and-choose process; it requires an intelligent, comprehensive philosophy that incorporates all the core practices to produce a spiritual champion. With that in mind, we identified the proportion of today's born-again parents who perceive just six of those proven strategies to be very important in their own efforts—specifically, being consistent, screening their child's friends, sharing their own beliefs and spiritual practices, supervising media exposure, facilitating active participation in their community of faith, and intentionally shaping the child's worldview. The outcome is that a mere 11% of the born-again parents today fit the profile. (Note that these six do not constitute the entire slate of efforts practiced by parents who successfully raised spiritual champions.)

But saying those approaches are very important is different from regularly implementing those practices. If we then look at what percentage of parents regularly practice those six things, the figure drops to 4% of all born-again parents. If we expand the scope of the evaluation to include all American parents, the figure drops to a miniscule 1% of our current population of parents.

Clearly, the critical insights learned about raising spiritual champions by recent generations of parents who accomplished that feat has *not* been passed on or accepted by most of today's born-again Christian parents. Unfortunately, the outcome of this rejection of proven practices is easy to predict—and just as easy to observe in the marketplace.

Consider the implications of this reality. We are setting up our children for failure in life, effectively preventing them from achieving their potential in Christ. We are dooming the future church to be fewer in number and less powerful in its impact on society. And we are certainly disappointing our Father in Heaven through the lame and half-baked commitment that we, as parents, have made to raising spiritual champions for His kingdom.

WHAT PARENTS PRIORITIZE—AND HOW IT'S WORKING

Raising a spiritual champion takes a particular mindset. Because you do what you believe, your beliefs about parenting will have a substantial impact on the type of child you strive to raise. Upon examining how spiritually inclined, born-again parents are raising their children today, the research shows more than a few shocking deficiencies.[23]

- Born-again parents are surprisingly divided as to their highest priority in life. Overall, the two highest-rated priorities are protecting and providing for their family and raising their children to be committed to following Jesus Christ. But despite its high ranking, raising their children to be disciples was identified as their top priority by just one out of every four born-again Christian parents (27%). That means three out of four born-again parents have priorities they are pursuing that they consider to be more important than raising their children to be spiritual champions.

- Most born-again parents are not overly satisfied with the spiritual, moral, character, or worldview development of their children. Statistically, between 15% and 23% of all born-again parents are very satisfied with their child's development in any of those areas. Interestingly, born-again parents are less satisfied with their child's well-being in every one of the nine dimensions studied than are other parents.

- Just six out of ten born-again parents (58%) contend that they, as the parents, have the primary responsibility for the spiritual development of their children. About one out of every four (23%) assign that responsibility to churches, with the remaining two out of ten distributing the responsibility across relatives, schools, peers, media, the community, and government.

- Oddly, born-again parents are more likely to claim the primary responsibility for the morals and values of their children than they are to accept that responsibility for the shaping of the spirituality and worldview.

- Barely half of born-again parents (53%) argue that they have the primary responsibility for their child's worldview development. About one-quarter of them assign that duty to the schools, far more frequent an answer than those who selected their church (3%).

- Asked what their children need to learn to be successful in life, born-again parents were more likely to list basic logic and reasoning, reading ability at a tenth-grade level or better, money management skills, and basic mathematics than any of the spiritual skills or insights offered as options.

- Although a worldview is something that their children will carry with them for the duration of their life and is a component that will determine every decision they make in life, a minority of born-again parents (41%) indicated that learning about worldview is necessary for their children to be successful in life. In fact, born-again parents were less likely than non-born-again parents to list worldview development as a component of life success for their children!

- Slightly more than half of all born-again parents rate themselves as "very effective" at shaping the spiritual development of their children. Fewer than two out of five parents describe their church as being "very effective" at this, and even fewer (just one-third) describe their extended family members as being "very effective."

- A mere three out of every ten born-again parents have spiritual goals for their children. Even fewer (two out of ten) have worldview-related goals for the young ones. These parents were more likely to have goals related to mental health, physical health, academic achievement, and athletic achievement than either spiritual or worldview development.

- Among the born-again parents who have established any goals for their children, they indicated they are more satisfied that their children are meeting the identified goals related to mental health, physical health, academic achievement, and athletic achievement than they are meeting the goals concerning spiritual or worldview development.

Among the born-again parents who said that introducing their children to the parent's spiritual beliefs and behaviors is a very important aspect of raising their youngsters, it is surprising how few religious activities most of them actually engage in with their children. There were only four practices that a majority regularly undertake with their children: praying together, worshiping together, reading the Bible together, and discussing the religious reasons behind the decisions they make.

Among the activities most of these parents do not do are studying the Bible together (as opposed to simply reading it), serving other people, providing the biblical reasons for disciplinary action, encouraging the child to keep a faith journal, facilitating regular times of confession, attending religious instruction classes or events, and screening the child's friends.

Before moving on with additional research, let me point out that several patterns emerged. One was that most of the born-again parents think they are very effective at helping their children develop a viable spiritual life. Yet it is striking that most of those same parents admit that they are unimpressed with the spiritual life of their children.

One likely explanation for this odd combination is that most born-again parents do not really think the spiritual component of their children's life is a big deal—at least not as big a deal as doing well in school, sports, or relationships. As people who are somewhat spiritually inclined themselves, they recognize that spiritual development must be on their list of duties, but the emerging sense is that their criteria for success regarding faith matters is not nearly as rigorous or carefully tracked as are the markers related to other dimensions of their child's life.

Another consistent finding was that the younger the parent, the less likely they were to describe spiritual and worldview development efforts and performance outcomes as very important. That corresponds to a pattern we see in our studies among Americans under the age of forty. The "spiritual but not religious" generations that make up the parenting segment of our population seem to be practicing what they preach—and they rarely preach about the importance of knowing, following, and pleasing Jesus.

PARENTS AND WORLDVIEW

As our surveys discovered, consistency in the Christian commitment of parents is sorely lacking. Not only is there an unremarkable degree of religious activity undertaken between parent and child (as described above), but three nationally representative surveys we conducted regarding the worldview of parents show that an overwhelming percentage of parents think of themselves as Christian (68%) but only 2% of them have a biblical worldview. That means when it comes to making decisions on everything in life—from relationships to morals, finances to values, public policy to lifestyle, and everything else imaginable—biblical principles are rarely a determinant in their decision-making process.[24] The vast bulk of America's parents—like the huge majority of other U.S. adults—are syncretists.[25] In other words, most parents make their moment-to-moment choices based upon a blend of ideas drawn from a variety of competing worldviews that form a unique synthesis of perspectives with which they are comfortable.

So even though two out of every three parents call themselves Christians, more than nine out of ten of those parents are syncretists. Which of those factors do you think has greater influence on their parenting decisions: their religious self-identification or their lifelong decision-making filter? Knowing that parents cannot give what they do not have—and that they do not have a deep, transforming commitment to biblical principles—clarifies why there are so few genuine disciples of Jesus in the nation, and why that number continues to decline. Because they are not disciples and they are ill-equipped to disciple their own offspring, the research is unequivocal in warning us that the future of the American church, as represented by the nation's children, is in peril.

Christianity has been the default faith for many generations in the United States. You have probably heard people refer to America as a "Christian nation." But that status does not correspond to the belief system of most people, including those who identify themselves as Christians and many who are active in Christian churches. In other words, claiming to be a Christian, or regularly participating in the life of a Christian church, does not make the person a Christian. Being a Christian is about consistently and fervently imitating Jesus Christ—believing and trusting in Him, thinking like Him, acting like Him, and serving Him in any way possible. That's what a biblical worldview enables a person to do.

So when we study the worldview of parents, the statistics indisputably and overwhelmingly show that most parents do not have a biblical perspective on most of the central beliefs of biblical Christianity. Here are just a few examples among the parents of children under the age of thirteen.

- Less than half believe that God is the all-knowing, all-powerful, perfect, and just Creator of the universe who still rules it today, or that the Bible is the true and reliable words of God.

- Just one-third contend that the purpose of life is to know, love, and serve God with all your heart, mind, strength, and soul; that the marriage of one man to one woman is God's only plan for humanity across all cultures of the world; or that God is the basis of all moral truth, as revealed in the Bible.

- Only one-quarter of parents believe that absolute moral truths exist and that they are the same for everyone, regardless of their circumstances; or that humans are born into sin and need Jesus to save them from the consequences; or that salvation is attainable solely by confessing your sins and accepting Jesus as your Lord and Savior; or that success in life can best be defined as consistent obedience to God; or that human life is sacred.

Removing these foundational truths from the Christian faith essentially guts the faith that God designed for humankind. Parents whose faith lacks full adherence to these perspectives cannot raise their children to be spiritual champions—or at least not Christian disciples. You cannot give what you do not have, and anyone who rejects these foundations does not have a valid, biblical Christian faith to share with their children.

CHANGING OUR APPROACH

There is an old expression, "If you keep doing what you've been doing, you'll keep getting what you've been getting." That may well summarize the state of discipleship in America. The Christian body is getting smaller and weaker by the decade because we have failed to adapt to the new strategies and tools deployed by our spiritual enemy,

Satan. The statistics are quite clear: Whatever we have been doing is not working. As uncomfortable as it may be, we must change our strategy and tactics.

Stop for a moment and reflect on what has been happening spiritually in America over the last forty-plus years.

While churches have merrily continued to focus on adults, the Evil One has switched course and now focuses on winning over those whose worldview and life choices are being shaped prior to reaching their teen years.

While churches have tried to combat the world by using their two hours per week spent with families through the traditional lecture-on-Sunday-plus-midweek-small-group plan, Satan has transitioned to using the media as his primary conduit for seducing Americans of all ages. The Christian community has stuck to the one-size-fits-all strategy while he has adopted a 500-channel, multiple-front media war campaign.

While parents have devoted themselves to making their children happy and providing a comfortable lifestyle for them, Satan has used those distractions to separate us from the life of simplicity, service, example, and consequent persecution that characterizes Jesus's model.

While parents and cultural leaders have proclaimed victory and superiority by pointing to evaluations that show our children to be getting high grades, competitive test scores, sports trophies, and musical accolades, Satan has laughed his head off, knowing that we have refused to measure our (lack of) production of spiritual fruit.

He probably sighs with deep satisfaction every time he studies the latest national statistics concerning violence, sexuality, morality, financial debt, and emotional trauma. In a world where you get what you measure, we have measured things that make us self-congratulatory at the expense of the things that matter.

In the 1975 movie *Monty Python and the Holy Grail* by the British comedy troupe Monty Python,[26] one of my favorite scenes is when the hero (King Arthur) battles the evil Black Knight in the forest. After a brief sword skirmish, Arthur slices off the left arm of his adversary. The Black Knight laughs it off and proclaims, "'Tis but a scratch. . . . I've had worse."

They battle on, and Arthur cuts off the Black Knight's other arm. The profusely bleeding Black Knight defiantly replies, "It's just a flesh wound." Next, Arthur cuts off his opponent's right leg. Defiantly, while hopping on one leg, the Knight proclaims, "I am invincible."

Eager to move on down the path, but still obstructed by his snarling, flailing enemy, Arthur finally severs the remaining leg and moves past him. Perseverant to the end, the Black Knight calls out after the victorious king, issuing a final challenge: "I'll bite your legs off."

For years, the sheer absurdity of that scene has caused me to laugh out loud. This time, however, I felt a sense of nausea, not from the cartoonish violence depicted in the scene, but upon realizing that the Black Knight's reactions are analogous to the ridiculous responses of the Christian body in America as we watch our enemy seduce and twist the minds of our innocent children. Yes, they are growing up amidst a spiritual battle for their minds, hearts, and souls, and we are failing to alert them to, and prepare them for, the battle.

We do not have the luxury of another generation's worth of time to ponder our predicament. We must act decisively and courageously now. The data regarding worldview and the associated moral and spiritual choices Americans are making have been screaming, "Emergency!" for decades. Today we are at the precipice of irreversible self-destruction.

The appallingly tiny incidence of biblical worldview among every age group in our society says it all, declining from the highest-but-anemic level among our oldest adults (8% among those sixty-five or older), to middle-aged adults (5% among those fifty to sixty-four years of age), to frighteningly low levels among adults thirty-to-forty-nine years old (3%) and those eighteen-to-twenty-nine (1%). The barely there proportion remains a paltry 1% among current teenagers.[27]

You do not need a doctorate in statistics to recognize the pattern or what it portends for the church and our nation, much less the spiritually frail individuals throughout our country.

How low does the incidence have to go before we admit that we have an existential crisis and must immediately get serious about discipling our children? Or does the extremely low biblical worldview incidence among adults—especially among those who are parents—mean we just don't care? Are we willing to accept defeat in this world and mindlessly wait until we die, believing that at least we guaranteed our own salvation by reciting the sinner's prayer and then wishing our children well on their spiritual journey?

If you love your child(ren), you cannot simply stand by and watch them, and their generation, forge a pathway toward eternal pain and suffering—all because you are unwilling to follow Jesus's command to make disciples and to follow His instructions on how to do so. We cannot spend our last years on the planet blaming someone else—the parents blame the local church, churches blame the culture, children blame their parents, and so forth—in an endless and indefensible round-robin of finger-pointing.

You are not reading this by accident. God is calling out to you, urging you to recognize that you are part of the solution. If you refuse to do your part, know that innocent people—yes, even family members—will suffer because of your untenable decision. But also, rejoice if you commit yourself to bringing about the radical change that must happen if we are to be the church and spread the good news in ways that allow God's Holy Spirit to use you as an agent of transformation.

Let's consider how we can turn things around without compromising the gospel. It has been compromised enough.

03

DISCIPLE-MAKING, YES—BUT WHY DISCIPLE CHILDREN?

ver the last three decades, the ministry strategy of American church-es has shifted in several significant ways. For starters, ministry success has been redefined, focusing on indicators such as attendance, donations, and number of programs available.[28] Activity and outcomes related to discipleship or to the spiritual development of children are rarely evaluated.[29] The emphasis reflected in the prevailing measurement criteria used by churches is telling; after all, you get what you measure.

Second, churches have eliminated most of the ministry programs and events that were commonplace for decades. Most Protestant churches around the nation have eliminated their midweek services, adult Sunday school, and many of their community outreach programs. The new regimen acquiesces to the busyness of people's lives by "simplifying" and consolidating their church-related expectations. Someone who attends a Sunday morning service, participates in a small group, and donates a significant amount of money to the church is now considered to be deeply committed.

Perhaps the most important shift of all, however, has been the reduced emphasis on ministering to children. That transition, in turn, has reinforced an unfortunate message to church people: Discipleship is ministry germane to adults. Ministry to children is a combination of giving their parents peace of mind with no distractions during church meetings, while providing some positive religious experiences to the children in their classes.

This follows the general shift in thinking about Christian discipleship: it is for the benefit of adults. The unstated ministry philosophy of many churches these days—a perspective also embraced by many churchgoing parents—could be indelicately summarized as follows:

- Attract children to the children's ministry, making them feel safe, happy, and comfortable. They will hear Bible stories and participate in child-oriented activities like singing, arts, and crafts. Ministry success is having children who want to return to the church for similar experiences, and parents who are confident their child is well cared for and having a good time in a Christian context.

- Attract teenagers to the youth ministry by providing an environment that promotes feeling comfortable, having fun, making friends, and hearing how the Bible is relevant to current cultural issues and personal life struggles. Success is the student feeling safe, accepted, and connected, and their parents feeling confident that their teen is in a secure and supportive religious environment.

- Attract parents and other adults to the church to be present for worship activities and to be exposed to biblical content through preaching. That information is reinforced through church-guided small group participation and engagement with other church programs of their choice. Successful ministry to those adults is evidenced by their regular attendance, note-taking or attentiveness during sermons, consistent giving to meet the church's financial needs, a sense of community achieved through a small-group experience, and the willingness to invite other adults and families to attend the church.

Forgive my directness in saying this, but churches all too often use children as bait to attract the desired catch of the day—parents. In other words, many churches view ministry to children not as the heartbeat of the entire ministry as much as a church growth inducement. The children's program is not viewed as the church's primary impact ministry; it is considered a reservoir for holding onto children until they mature into "discipleship material."

That perspective is exemplified by comments such as those by one pastor of children's ministry who described his congregation's ministry to children as "the growth engine" of his church. He went on to proclaim that a "thriving children's ministry where kids look forward to attending on Sunday"—that is, a program whose success is measured by repeat attendance—will entice "parents and grandparents [to] follow suit," meaning they will come back time and again. In other words, keep the kids happy, and you can snag the adults who naively assume that the minimal spiritual needs of their child are being satisfied.[30]

Across the nation, discipleship is frequently mentioned by church leaders but is neither an intentional nor evaluated aspect of the ministry. And it is rarely assumed by churches—or parents—that children should be intentionally and actively trained to be followers of Jesus Christ beyond adopting basic "Christian" attitudes and attributes such as "being a good person," "following the Ten Commandments," "believing in God," and "praying to God" during times of difficulty or need.

It is amazing how many parents bring their infant or young child to a local church to experience a dedication ceremony at which the church leaders, parents, and congregants publicly vow that they will work together to raise that child in the Christian faith, with the goal of becoming a committed follower of Jesus Christ.

And then we mark time with them for the next decade or more.

Why? It is not that our church leaders want to delay the spiritual formation of our children. It is not that parents want to withhold spiritual blessings and resources from their children.

It is largely because parents and church leaders do not believe that someone can become a true disciple of Jesus until they are old enough to reason and make important decisions. Nationally, the body of Christ rejects the scriptural idea that children are born as spiritual beings and need to be prepared for spiritual battle at an early age.

If you do not want to accept the cultural evidence of the significance of children, the Bible is very clear in that regard. We may not take the spiritual life and development of children seriously, but it is not because God has failed to exhort us to do so.

For instance, King David wrote that children are capable of describing the strength of God and to thereby silence His enemies.[31] They are able to hear and discern God's voice, and to be called upon by Him to represent the Lord in courageous ways.[32] They not only know God with humility and sincerity, but also exhibit an exemplary degree of trust in Him.[33]

Paul actually modeled the importance of teaching children spiritual truth when he wrote directly to them about their thoughts and actions.[34]

Maybe a comparison will help. In the typical American family, parents provide some behavioral rules and moral teachings to their children. They teach their children manners, civility, appropriate language, grooming, and basic elements of right and wrong behavior. In most cases, parents indicate the importance of those teachings through both modeling and the application of disciplinary measures for a child's refusal to live within the prescribed boundaries. If we define discipleship as imitating the belief and behavioral patterns of one's mentor, then we can say that parents are discipling their children, with themselves as the mentor to be mimicked.[35]

However, when it comes to the spiritual discipleship of children—identifying Jesus Christ as the mentor to emulate, based upon His principles and commands provided in the Bible—neither parents nor our churches seem to believe that children are capable of flourishing within that spiritual discipleship process. Most Christian parents, who have the biblical obligation to spiritually equip their children, believe they fulfill that duty simply by enrolling the children in a Sunday school class. Those same parents delay any substantive discipling process until their child is in their teens or twenties.

In the interim, the single hour each week that a child might have in a church program is essentially a soft introduction to the possibility of some future, church-based spiritual formation activity that they may choose to pursue.

A VULNERABLE TIME

The American musician and poet, Bob Dylan, won a Nobel Prize in literature in addition to numerous Grammy Awards for his creative work. One of his more popular songs among Christians is a simple but insightful song entitled "(You) Gotta Serve Somebody."[36] In that song, Dylan reminds us of a fundamental biblical concept: Everyone, at all times, is making the choice of whom they will serve in any given moment and situation. As the chorus of the song informs, you might choose to serve Satan, or you might choose to serve the Lord, but ultimately your actions cannot help but serve someone and their agenda.

Anyone who makes a decision does so with the intent of satisfying the person to whom they answer or whom they have chosen to emulate. That is every bit as true for children as it is for adults. And it is the underlying reason for world leaders over the course of centuries making comments such as, "Give me a child until the age of seven, and they will be mine for the rest of their lives."

While this statement was originally attributed to Aristotle, variations on that statement have been made by totalitarian political leaders as diverse as Vladimir Lenin, Benito Mussolini, Adolf Hitler, Joseph Stalin, and Mao Tse-Tung.

But the same philosophy has also been promoted by compassionate religious leaders like Saint Ignatius of Loyola and Saint Francis Xavier. The compelling point made by all these leaders is that the ideas planted in the minds and hearts of children during their most impressionable years have staying power. In fact, that concept has been a foundational idea driving the Jesuit investment in educating children for several hundred years.

My own research on worldview development has shown this still to be true, although the radical changes in culture from times past suggest that the developmental process covers an extended period of time these days.

But that is just one of the four phases of worldview experience in American life that we identified. Children do not realize that they are creating a blueprint for the rest of their life; they are simply trying to make sense of life, make good choices, and learn from each of those experiences. The positives and negatives they take away from their choices enable them to piece together a patchwork of beliefs that they translate into a behavioral code.

An outsider looking in at their worldview might be tempted to critique it as inconsistent and internally contradictory. The child, though, is unconcerned about the philosophical purity of their choices. They are simply trying to satisfy a variety of needs, desires, expectations, and opportunities by selecting options that seem optimal.

As they move through their teens and twenties, they do not have as great a need to fill holes in their life-response grid; by this time they are optimizing the possibilities. Thus, during this second phase of their worldview development, their goal is to constantly test and perfect their philosophy of life, seeking to confirm the validity and reliability of the beliefs and behaviors that got them through their early years to now owning a more refined approach to life.

Once they are confident that their worldview fits who they see themselves as being and will support the kind of life they want to lead, they enter a third worldview phase in which they become an evangelist for their worldview. Their self-assurance increases as others adopt the same points of view and behaviors they champion.

The final worldview phase is one of reflection. This typically occurs when a person is in their sixties and beyond. During this period, they evaluate how well their worldview has served them, determined by its consistency with who they wanted to be and how adequately it enabled them to live the life they sought. Those reflections become most valuable as they discuss such matters with young people, such as their grandchildren or great grandchildren.

Given that timeline, it is clear that when it comes to worldview, the most important period in a person's life is during the formative childhood years. In like manner, then, the most decisive time for us to influence someone regarding beliefs and behaviors related to God, I Christ, the Bible, truth, salvation, morality, life purpose, success, and the like—key components of our worldview—is during those early childhood years.

COMPETITION FOR INFLUENCE

But my research has also revealed that even if you want to be the chief agent of influence in a child's life—especially related to their moral and spiritual development—your role as a chief influencer is far from assured. Our research suggests that parents are among the six most dominant sources of influence on the minds and hearts of children. However, we also learned that as the child progresses through their development period, parents are usually not the primary source of impact, and their influence wanes as the child ages.

Who—or what—has the greatest impact? The arts and entertainment media to which our children are exposed. Through a variety of media—television, movies, social media, recorded music, books, video games, radio and audio streaming, and short-form videos—thousands upon thousands of moral and spiritual messages are sent directly to our children every single day.

While there does not appear to be a coordinated effort to foist a particular worldview upon our children, it is just as clear that a biblical worldview is rarely conveyed to young people through those media. More often than not, the philosophical foundation of the messages conveyed is either that there is no supreme being (e.g., the God of Israel) or that the recipient of the message is their own deity.

Naturally, the implications of that philosophy are deep and dramatic in relation to ideas about morality, meaning and purpose, success, life after death, human nature, and so on. With children bombarded with what experts estimate to be hundreds of unbiblical messages from the arts and entertainment sector every day, cutting through that ocean of moral garbage is exceedingly difficult. There is just too much thematic noise for children to receive a clear call to God's ways.

It is helpful, though, to stop for a moment and ask why the media are so intent on overwhelming children with their messaging. After all, kids control very little money; they have no tangible political power; they are generally incapable of initiating a movement or rallying a significant group of people; and they have a limited voice and capacity to articulate a position in ways that will stir and influence society. But the media recognize what Aristotle, Hitler, Ignatius of Loyola, and others have long touted: Win over children when they are young, and you have a loyal follower for life.

Other major players in the effort to influence children include family, especially parents; schools; peers; and the government, through its laws and policies. Together with arts and entertainment media, these six power players have an estimated 70% or so of the influence on the way children will understand and respond to the world. Churches typically have so little influence on the worldview of children that they do not rate among the top ten influence agents in a typical child's life.[37]

Without meaning to be harsh or judgmental, the research seems to suggest that while churches (and, to a large extent, families) have been focused on making children feel happy and emotionally secure, the entertainment media and government, in particular, have been intent on using their content to both establish a dominant worldview in the minds and hearts of America's children. To their credit—and our detriment—they have largely succeeded.

But how have they done that?

There are several elements that seem obvious. One is that they used the most effective methods of communication. That means they have communicated their perspectives through *stories* that are accessible to the mind of the intended audience. They have repeated their philosophies, over and over, as if they are proven and accepted truths. That act of *repetition* has served to make their ideas seem to be the norm rather than a mere theory or preference.

They have garnered *peer acceptance* of those messages and developed associated tools that have further amplified those messages. In doing so, they managed to generate sufficient momentum to minimize audience doubts and questions about those philosophies.

What questions are being raised and answered - most often from an unbiblical perspective - by those who are creating the mass media that is naively absorbed by our children? The very same questions that an effective ministry to children addresses!

- How did I get here? Where did I come from? (Creation).

- Who am I? Why do I exist? (Purpose).

- What really matters in life? What is most important? (Success).

- Who is in charge? Who am I supposed to answer to? (Authority).

- Do relationships matter? Which ones? (Belonging).

- How do I know how I'm doing? (Standards).

- What can I do to maximize pleasure and minimize pain? (Boundaries).

- What will happen to me if I die? (Salvation).

Realistically, nobody waits until their teens or twenties to get satisfying answers to these questions. Children are asking and pondering these matters because they want—no, they *need*—to know the answers. When properly communicated, children can grasp the answers provided and apply them in their daily decisions. Unfortunately, most children are receiving an avalanche of errant perspectives from secular people who do not care about the lives of our children and certainly do not accept the Bible as a source of truth and guidance. Just as many social institutions do, they view our children as a means to an end.

REFOCUSING ON DISCIPLING CHILDREN

Don't lose sight of the fact that a one-year-old has a worldview vacuum that will be filled over her first decade of existence. She cannot survive and flourish, as God wants her to, without developing answers to the big questions of life. She will not hunt for theological arguments; she needs practical, child-friendly ways of understanding how life works, what it's about, and her place in it.

The world is rushing to her doorstep—or, more accurately, her tablet, television screen, smartphone, and books. To win her soul, it is hugely advantageous to get there first and provide the truth that will transform her rapidly maturing mind and heart. This is one of those pressure-packed challenges where you cannot procrastinate. Usually, whoever addresses her spiritual and moral needs first, wins.

The Scriptures command us to "direct your children onto the right path, and when they are older, they will not leave it."[38] We cannot afford to fail at this task, either by leaving it in the hands of others or by doing an ineffective job of properly educating our children in matters of faith. If we do a poor job, the Scriptures warn us what the outcome will be: "You will always harvest what you plant."[39]

SECTION TWO

THE FOUR PRACTICES OF A DISCIPLE

Nobody is born a disciple. Our human nature is selfish and therefore prone to sin. Our natural inclination, which is evident even as infants, is to believe and live as if the world revolves around us. To be a disciple of something or someone else is an act of will.

Anyone who is a genuine disciple of Jesus Christ had to work at becoming His follower. Becoming an imitator of Christ does not happen naturally or easily; it is an intentional choice and a course of transformation that takes time and effort.

As previously documented, most American adults describe themselves as Christians. But appropriating the label "Christian" and living in a Christlike manner are two divergent realities. The typical commitment to Christ is lax and inconsistent among most self-identified Christians. Relatively few of them are even aware of their spiritual inadequacies. Not many choose to immerse themselves in an intensive commitment to become a more dedicated and proficient disciple. That ambivalence about their spiritual condition is a major reason why most parents (and, by extension, relatives, pastors, and teachers) do not invest much in the discipling of children.

Those who become serious disciples of Christ typically engage in four practices that lead them to a deeper spiritual life. The next four chapters describe these practices, particularly in relation to raising children to become spiritual champions.

1. Making a life-defining *commitment* to be a disciple of Jesus

2. Accepting the *biblical principles and commands* that lead to becoming a disciple

3. Adopting the *lifestyle* of a disciple—obedience through the application of beliefs

4. Inviting personal *accountability* and stability—through assessing what matters, reinforcing growth, and celebrating disciplehood

If you want a roadmap for how to raise a child to be a spiritual champion, these four practices offer a well-traveled pathway en route to a successful outcome. Let's dig into each of these four practices to understand what they require.

04
DISCIPLE-MAKING PRACTICE #1 MAKE A LIFE-DEFINING COMMITMENT TO JESUS

Think about how being a devoted follower of someone works.

We live in a celebrity-obsessed culture, so let's take the example of being a follower of a popular singer. You start by gaining exposure to her music and decide to get more deeply acquainted with her music and career. You listen to more songs. Duly impressed, you dive a bit deeper, downloading more of her songs into your music archives, or maybe you set up a channel devoted to her songs on your favorite streaming platform. Curious for more, you watch some videos of her performances.

Her music becomes a regular part of your life. When you discover that she's on tour and will be coming to your area, you shell out big bucks to get good seats to experience her talent in person. As a big fan of her artistry, you read every article about her you can find. In short, you pursue every opportunity to digest information about her and to enjoy whatever she produces.

But that's not enough. When she switches out her look with a new hairstyle and dies her locks purple, you follow suit. You discover that she practices yoga each morning, so begin your own yoga regimen. In an interview, she discusses her devotion to Kabbalah, a form of Jewish mysticism, which you then begin to practice. Noticing her unusually gaunt frame, you scour the internet and learn she is a vegan, causing you to mimic her diet.

You have become more than just a fan. You are a true follower, altering a significant slice of your lifestyle to be connected to her artistry and life.

Or maybe your obsession is not with a person, but rather a product. A popular example is weight-loss products or programs. It is estimated that more than 120 million Americans invest in weight-loss efforts in a typical year.[40] It is a common desire to not be overweight, so you research the alternatives and choose one particular weight-loss program. The program you choose lays out an exercise regimen to follow, which you engage in regularly. The program prescribes a special diet, so you stop eating some of the foods you enjoy and replace them with foods you would never have considered prior to your determination to lose weight.

You weigh yourself every morning and keep careful records of how you're doing. You alter your schedule to fit with the requirements of the program, including increasing the amount of sleep you get each night. As you begin to see positive results, you intensify your efforts. You are becoming a different person because of your determination to lose weight, no matter what it takes.

Your devotion to the program, and the results it delivers, has altered many facets of your life. It is hard work to maintain the commitment, but you persist because you are so pleased with the results. You speak highly of the program and its benefits to other people you know who might be interested. You have become a devoted follower of that program, a disciple of that system.

It's no different with your spiritual life. Most people initiate their pathway to becoming a real disciple of Jesus by "taking a test drive"— sampling what the Christian life has to offer. That journey can start anywhere: reading the Bible, attending a church service, watching a television preacher, befriending, and carefully observing the life of an unabashed Jesus follower, praying to see if God is real enough to answer your prayers, or any of a multitude of other entry points.

It is a little different if you are targeting a child to become a disciple of the Lord. In that case, your job is to be the model and mentor for the child. Hopefully, you will not be the only one—most Christians mature into devoted followers in response to the spiritual investment of many Christians along the way—but it is common for disciples to have at least one particular individual who focuses on them and commits themselves to help that child to grow. For most children, that catalytic partner will be a parent, grandparent, teacher, coach, or pastor.

It is a huge privilege to become a spiritual mentor to anyone, but especially to a child. That engagement brings joy to God and enhanced life to the child. But getting the process off the ground might seem quite onerous. How do you initiate that adventure? What are the guideposts for that journey? How do you know if things are going well?

Generally speaking, the best approach is organic. Rather than trying to orchestrate situations to foster the desired outcome, start by being tangentially involved in the spiritual environment of the child, then progress to building a genuine relationship with the child and allowing the Lord to orchestrate the process. But we'll dive into that more deeply in the next chapter. Before that, let's get a grasp on some other factors.

From the beginning, it helps to know what you're trying to facilitate in the child's life—and what you both agree upon as the ideal outcome for the child. Not surprisingly, Jesus provides a helping hand in the process by defining what it means to be His disciple. That is the outcome to keep in mind as you assist any child in reaching their God-given purpose.

DEFINING DISCIPLESHIP

Being a genuine disciple starts with obedience. While mentoring His disciples, Jesus told them, "You are truly my disciples if you remain faithful to my teachings."[41] The first sign of a commitment to being His disciple is consistently obeying His commands and principles.

Why obey His teachings? Because He provided them so we may flourish in life.

The entire Bible is not an outdated parcel of restrictions that destroy the chance of enjoying life. The teachings God offers are designed to set us up for success and joy. Rather than grudgingly learning and dutifully living by the letter of the law, we fare best when we gratefully adopt and passionately carry out His best plan for us.

Jesus commonly reminded His followers about the importance of obedience to God's laws. When He gave the Great Commission, the portion of it that we often ignore, verse 20, tells us, "Teach these new disciples to obey all the commands I have given you."[42]

This was consistent with His teaching during the Sermon on the Mount, when He noted, "Anyone who obeys God's laws and teaches them will be called great in the Kingdom of Heaven. . . . But anyone who hears my teaching and doesn't obey it is foolish, like a person who builds a house on sand."[43]

Of course, you cannot fully obey His commands if you do not know what they are. Obedience therefore demands knowledge of the Scriptures. As a disciple-maker, you must know the principles and commands of God so that you may thoroughly follow them, but also so that when you disciple others, you are equipping them for complete obedience.

Being a disciple is not just about obedience, though. Jesus went on to inform His followers that a real disciple is someone who loves other disciples. There is no competition or jealousy involved; instead, disciples are enthusiastic about being part of a community of fellow forgiven sinners who are also on the journey to wholeness through devotion to the Master.

Gratefully and humbly belonging to a community of sojourners will capture the attention of the world around us. Jesus told His followers, "Your love for one another will prove to the world that you are my disciples."[44]

The apostle Paul often taught about the importance of practical demonstrations of love to each other. For example, he exhorted his followers in Ephesus and Colossae to treat each other with love as a reflection of the love Christ had shown to them.[45] Such acceptance and mutual support are increasingly rare in today's society. A community built on forbearance and empathetic relationships will startle the world and realign your own life.

When a person consistently obeys Jesus's ways and exudes genuine love of other believers, they will stand out from the crowd because they are not living for personal advantage and advancement. Beyond that selfless lifestyle, though, Jesus explained that a true disciple, in addition to demonstrating obedience and love, produces spiritual fruit. He alluded to the necessity of a disciple producing positive outcomes when He taught, "When you produce much fruit, you are my true disciples. This brings great glory to my Father."[46]

Delivering positive, tangible outcomes for the kingdom of God is often an outgrowth of the personal transformation that discipleship introduces, as evidenced by the fruit of the Spirit in your life: love, joy, peace, patience, kindness, goodness, faithfulness, gentleness, and self-control.[47] Or it might be human fruit that serves to advance the kingdom of God, i.e., new disciples.

In a different setting, Jesus also described disciples differently. As the crowds around Him were multiplying in size, He may have been concerned that those people did not understand the sacrifice and hardships involved in abandoning the world in favor of joining God's kingdom. His words must have startled more than a few.

> A large crowd was following Jesus. He turned around and said to them, "If you want to be my disciple, you must, by comparison, hate everyone else—your father and mother, wife and children, brothers and sisters—yes, even your own life. Otherwise, you cannot be my disciple. And if you do not carry your own cross and follow me, you cannot be my disciple. But don't begin until you count the cost."[48]

Jesus was not striving to attract larger crowds; He was after repentant and devout hearts. He chose His words carefully, and the allusion to carrying one's own cross was a culturally meaningfully reference to criminals having to carry their cross to their own crucifixion under the Roman system of justice. It was a sign of submission to authority and a warning that there is a substantial cost required of those who broke from the prevailing laws and principles of Roman rule. In like manner, anyone who hopes to be a citizen of the kingdom of God must surrender their authority to Him and understand the personal toll their submission will take over the course of their life.

Disciples, then, could be described as people whose purpose in life conforms to the Great Commandment: to know, love, and serve God with all their heart and soul, mind, and strength. A different way of describing a disciple is someone who thinks like Jesus, which enables them to act like Jesus, producing someone who therefore lives like Jesus.

Motivating children to desire the status of *disciple of Jesus* is perhaps best accomplished by sharing a compelling vision of the Christian life. That vision is founded on knowing and carrying out God's will, belonging to a community of like-minded followers, and carrying out the lifestyle that Jesus modeled. That is a vision built upon identifying with Christ, living like Him, voluntarily sacrificing everything to be His follower, and looking forward to spending eternity with Him. Your call to action will be far more persuasive if you are modeling that lifestyle for them.

COMMITTING TO AN IDENTITY

Recent years have spotlighted the controversies related to personal identity. It is difficult to get through the day's news without encountering at least one significant story related to conflict concerning laws and experiences regarding sexual, racial, or other forms of personal identity.

Even for those who do not wrestle with issues of sexual or racial identity, your sense of identity is a big deal. You make decisions every day based on what you believe about yourself. If you believe you are physically weak, you won't place yourself in situations that threaten your safety or well-being. If you believe you are ignorant, you probably will not challenge those who are more educated or seem to be well informed. If you accept people saying that you are unattractive, you are less likely to seek the company of those who are deemed handsome or beautiful. In some ways, identity is destiny because we generally limit our options based on our sense of self.

Discipleship is very deeply related to identity—trading in the identity the world wants us to embrace, or wants to hang on us, in favor of the identity we adopt when we become a disciple of Jesus. Notice that when we make that exchange, we are rejecting the values of the world in favor of the values of God.

The world identifies us by our intelligence, appearance, race, family, political ideology, wealth, and similar factors. God identifies us by our surrender to Him and our commitment to Jesus—not just a verbal acknowledgment of His Son, but the depth of our determination to be like Him.

Identifying with Christ is a huge commitment, with grand implications—and it usually takes some getting used to. And to be honest, anyone who openly and unashamedly identifies as a devoted follower of Jesus Christ at this moment in America's history is likely to face widespread disapproval and even overt hostility from some detractors.

Jesus was never coy about that possibility. He was well aware that His presence, and our decision to align with Him, would be controversial. He cautioned His followers that persecution from the world was part of the price of following Him. As He and the early disciples discovered, the world hated Him so much that they murdered Him. Why should those who publicly and proudly proclaim Him to be their king expect to be any less despised and abused?

But on the other hand, identifying as a Christ-follower adds many exciting and rewarding facets to your identity. The children we disciple need to grasp the fullness of that identity. Disciples are reconstituted by God, after they commit to Christ, in the ways listed below.

- You became a completely *new creation*. Who you are before following Jesus—a citizen of the world and its ways—dies as you embrace your rebirth through Jesus, becoming a *citizen of Heaven* (2 Corinthians 5:17; Ephesians 2:19).

- You are *forgiven* by the grace of God through Jesus Christ. You are spiritually *born again*. You are saved from the consequences of your sin, enabling Jesus to live in you and through you, via His Holy Spirit. With your sins crucified, you are no longer enslaved to your natural, sinful nature; you are liberated to act in harmony with the life principles He gave you (John 1:12; Romans 6:6; 8:1; 10:9–10; 1 Corinthians 6:17; Galatians 2:20; Ephesians 1:7).

- You are a *child of God*, loved by your heavenly Father—lavishly (Galatians 3:26; 1 John 3:1).

- You are *transformed*. Your mind is renewed, and you are righteous and holy. That transformation brings you boldness and confidence (Romans 12:2; Ephesians 3:12; 4:24).

- You are a *creature of God*, designed to be His *servant* by performing good things for His glory and in His ways. As His servant you are an *ambassador* of His love and grace, a *doer of His will*, and honored to be a *worshipper* of the King (2 Corinthians 5:20; 9:8; Ephesians 2:10; Philippians 2:9–11; 1 Peter 2:9).

- You become a *spiritual warrior* commissioned to fight the good fight of faith on behalf of our Creator and Savior (Zephaniah 3:17; Philippians 1:27; 1 Timothy 6:12; 1 Peter 5:8–10).

That's a completely different profile than most people—even, according to the research, most born-again Christians—carry in their mind and heart about themselves. But that's the biblical profile of a true disciple. And that's the mindset you, as a disciple-maker, are called to help emerging followers of Jesus to grasp and adopt for themselves. Identity is a powerful motivator for how we live and what we commit to.

As we disciple children, this is the identity they must understand and embrace. One of the foundational life principles I've discovered after interviews with more than one million Americans over the last four decades is that *you do what you believe.* You carry out what you believe about yourself. You act in harmony with what you believe about God or other spiritual entities and principles.

The role of disciple is a difficult role, akin to that of a sergeant in boot camp. You must take raw talent and abilities and mold them into a recognizable and desirable product. As you ponder how anyone could possibly shape a one- or two- or six-year-old into a disciple of Christ—or if you doubt that such early-life experiences will make a difference in who the child becomes—remember that television ads, social media shorts, online videos, musical lyrics, board books, peer conversations, teacher comments, and the behavior of sports stars and entertainment celebrities are just a few examples of the dozens of inputs that are shaping the minds and hearts of the children in your midst today. Those influential elements are planting many seeds in the minds and hearts of children—seeds about identity, purpose, authority, morality, success, and so much more.

Influential messages and examples, no matter where they come from, fill a vacuum that exists in children—a gaping hole of understanding that must be filled for the child to move forward with her life. But those messages and examples are more than a stop-gap measure; they are also a vital part of the spiritual war that is taking place around us. Someone will fill that vacuum, and they'll fill it with the ideas they believe are right. And they will seek to have children imitate them and accept their ideas—factors that will form the child's ultimate commitments and identity.

Given that reality, think about this.

If the child you are discipling believes that because of her understanding of and relationship with God, she has been created by Him as His beloved child on Earth and will eventually live forever with Him thanks to the saving grace of Jesus, then she will spend every day of her life differently than would have otherwise been the case.

As a self-aware disciple of the Lord, she will think about people and our world differently because her mind has been renewed by God. She will feel differently about people and their plight because her heart has been touched by the profound love of God.

She will behave unlike most of her peers because she longs to be popular in the eyes of Jesus Christ, and Him alone. She wants to imitate Jesus. She knows she is holy, that is, set apart from the rest, called to something higher and greater, and capable of achieving it because she operates in the power of the Spirit, not the self.

She is not embarrassed to think of herself—or be referred to—as a servant of God. No, she feels honored to have the honor of devoting her life to serving Him through her choices and actions. And, far from naïve, she recognizes that life is warfare. It cannot be avoided, and everybody takes a side in that eternal spiritual conflict. She is a spiritual warrior aligned with God, a declared enemy of Satan.

Because of her commitments to her heavenly Father, she will be loved by some, misunderstood by most, shunned by more than a few of her peers, and actually hated by many people—simply because she seeks to be His ambassador in a corrupt and evil world. There will be moments of doubt and pain, but she wouldn't have it any other way.

Trials, tribulations, tests, and even persecution won't stop her. She is a devoted disciple of Jesus Christ, and nothing can change that.

Let me remind you that the foundations of that conviction start to develop as early as fifteen to eighteen months of age. Her mindset is likely to be fully developed before she reaches the age of thirteen. It can be changed, but based on the data I have been collecting and analyzing for more than forty years, it is not likely to change much, if at all, after the age of thirteen. Yes, this is a race with gargantuan implications for the child and her world.

A RELATIONAL COMMITMENT

Contrary to common belief, disciples do not emerge from winning the attendance pin at church, listening to enough sermons, or participating in small groups or Sunday school classes.

Yet learning biblical principles from sermons can provide valuable insights and motivation that support becoming a disciple. And participating in faith-related group experiences can connect you to a community of like-minded people who will encourage and support you in your quest to becoming a follower of Jesus.

The research indicates, however, that those activities are secondary when it comes to becoming a true disciple of the Lord.

As the example given by Jesus shows, discipleship is a relational endeavor. My studies have consistently confirmed that people almost always become disciples because one, or a series of followers led them on a deeper journey toward Christ. That relationship between discipler and disciple-in-process is crucial to the outcome of the latter individual.

For this process to be productive, a child must be allowed by his or her parents to be involved in a faith-driven relationship with a disciple. That disciple might be the child's parent(s), a grandparent or other relative, a pastor or church leader, a teacher, a peer, or someone else who has proven to be a committed and mature follower of Jesus.

The relationship must be allowed to unfold based on the spiritual needs of the disciple-to-be. It is not unheard of for overly protective parents to squelch an otherwise healthy and productive discipleship connection. It is important for parents to be cautious and protective of their children, but not to be so overbearing or worried that their fears destroy the positive potential of a valuable discipleship connection.

The disciple-maker must also be willing to make commitments. Those include the following:

- **Serving Christ**. While many people think of discipling relationships being all about the humans involved, perhaps the most significant commitment is made to God. The analogy is Christian marriage.

  When a man and woman come before God and promise to take care of each other for the duration of their lives, it is a connection that includes God as well. The seriousness of discipleship may not be a "til death do us part" term, but it is similarly robust in that it connects three concerned parties—

the one who wants to follow Christ, the one who is following Christ and wants to help the emerging follower, and Christ Himself.

The disciple must therefore understand and consent to entering a discipling relationship as an act of spiritual service to Christ. The disciple is ultimately accountable to the Lord for what is done in the course of discipling a less spiritually mature follower of the Lord.

Sadly, unless the disciple has this depth of commitment to the relationship, it is easy to drop the connection when a better offer, personal difficulties, a busy schedule, or relational challenges enter the picture.

• **Building a solid relationship.** The discipler must mentally accept the idea that he or she is going to be spending a lot of quality time with their spiritual protégé. For that to work, the relationship with the protégé must be real.

That means genuinely caring about the child. It means making adequate time to keep the process moving forward at a healthy pace, knowing that it will require personal sacrifices and inconveniences.

The relationship will advance only if the mentor really listens to the child and responds with care and honesty. These factors will go a long way toward developing the most important component of a lasting and influential relationship—trust.

- **Investing personal resources**. A relationship designed to produce a disciple is much more than just hanging out and sharing some religious ideas or reading part of the Bible together. The discipler must invest personal resources in the process. Sufficient time to build and further the relationship is the most obvious resource—and perhaps the most frequently under-estimated element. Biblical knowledge and spiritual experiences are crucial for the disciple-making process to work. The willingness and ability to communicate both biblical information and personal life victories and defeats is an irreplaceable ingredient in the mix.

  God makes some people to be innately shy (for instance, yours truly is deeply introverted), but for a disciple-making effort to bear fruit, those who are shy or excessively humble must create a sufficiently safe connection to share anything and everything of value to the growth of the nascent disciple.

- **Implementing a solid plan**. Some adults who seek to disciple children figure because of their age, life experience, intelligence, and spiritual tenure they can wing it. Don't! The failure to drive the process forward through consistent reliance upon prayer, forethought, and preparation sets you up for a broken relationship and missed opportunities.

  Pastor Robert Schuller used to warn, "Those who fail to plan, plan to fail." A good plan that is faithfully executed will facilitate solid returns on your investment. Of course, you want to leave leeway for the Holy Spirit to guide you throughout the process, but even the Holy Spirit works more effectively when you seek His wisdom and guidance prior to engaging with your younger colleague.

A plan that is too rigid may squeeze the life and energy out of the process. But a plan that is too ill-formed is more likely to drain the relationship of trust and enthusiasm.

Also, realize that your plan must be built around who you are and the characteristics of the child you will coach. While a book like this can identify some attributes of successful discipling experiences, no author can define every step of your plan, regardless of the predictability of you and your disciple-to-be. If it were that cut-and-dried of a process, don't you think the Bible would have listed each step for us to follow? If everyone was to be discipled in exactly the same way, then why didn't Jesus use the same approach with each of the men He discipled, instead of treating Peter, James, John, and the rest of His crew as unique individuals who would benefit from a tailored process? Get to know your emerging disciple and create a process that will enable both of you to shine.

- **Using proven practices.** Having just warned against using a standardized set of procedures in your discipling effort, let me now identify some types of activities that will allow you to make progress based on how well you own and customize these tactics in your disciple-making adventure. These are elements that my studies have found to be crucial to successfully shaping potential disciples. These are also approaches that you'll find in the Bible—practices that were utilized by Jesus as He grew the body of believers, one by one.

- *Use the Bible as the basis* of your disciple-making efforts. The content you teach should be biblical principles and commands. The behaviors that you encourage and celebrate should be those valued in the Scriptures. We only know what a disciple is because of what the Bible tells us, and we should therefore stick to the precepts it divulges for our consideration and imitation.

- It is helpful to start the process by reflecting on *the grand narrative of the Christian faith*. Young people these days are taught to be sensitive to the big-picture perspective of how life works. Postmodernism, one of the most common worldviews promoted in the media to which youngsters are exposed, emphasizes identifying and scrutinizing the grand narrative of any philosophical underpinning.

- The grand narrative of biblical Christianity describes three epochs in human history: God's creation of the universe and humanity, the fall of humanity due to sin, and the restoration of the world through Jesus Christ.

Establishing those eras as touch points for future conversation is valuable.

○ In order to consistently and comprehensively think like Jesus, a person needs to embrace *a biblical worldview*. Everyone has a worldview from a very early age, but few people know what their worldview is, how it forms, or what elements comprise that perspective. There are many worldviews to choose from.

○ The biblical worldview is in short supply in America today; only 4% of adults and 2% of parents possess such a philosophy of life.[49] My recent research, however, has identified an easy and effective way to move down the pathway toward developing a biblical worldview—even among children. (That content—called *the seven cornerstones of the biblical worldview*—is described in the next chapter.) As you work with your emerging disciple, keep in mind that the seven cornerstones are an ideal starting point for building a solid, lifelong perspective.

○ The most effective means of growing disciples appears to be through *one-on-one coaching*.[50] You will hear this referred to as personal discipling, spiritual mentoring, biblical coaching, spiritual tutoring, Christian formation, and other phrases. What matters most is that there is a solid personal connection between a disciple and someone who is committed to becoming a disciple.

○ Other experiences—worship services, small groups, faith-related classes, community service projects, religious book clubs, and so forth—can add value to the process. But having a leader coaching a protégé has proven to be far more effective than any of the other events, programs, or approaches we have tested.

○ *Use stories and repeat key principles* on a regular basis. Most people—including children—recall stories better than a list of facts. Stories capture our imagination and help us to remember critical bits of information. Great teachers are able to weave stories into a more complex transfer of information to drive home beliefs, values, and behavioral principles. This is what Jesus did. He told stories that made a point without being heavy-handed in doing so.

○ Telling the same or similar stories multiple times strengthens recall of the key points. Have you ever noticed how much children enjoy watching the same videos over and over? It provides them a sense of comfort as well as pleasure at the same time that the underlying principles are being driven deeper into their mind and heart. You can exploit that practice for the benefit of your emerging disciple.

○ Telling stories isn't enough, though. A great discipler engages in *Socratic dialogue* with their protégé. That simply means that you address the central themes you wish to drive home through a series of questions about how your protégé experienced and interpreted the information to which they were exposed, and what lessons they can draw and apply from the material.

○ Being effective in Socratic conversations requires you to be both good at listening to what you are being told, and artfully translating the material into the conversation.

○ The beauty of Socratic conversations is that the protégé winds up owning the principles because they feel as if they arrived at those conclusions by themselves. They figure out the principles because the questions drive them to those conclusions. It takes practice to become comfortable and skilled at posing those kinds of questions and knowing how to field the off-track responses that sometimes arise, but it is a powerful process once you figure it out.

○ Talking about the truths and principles of the Christian life is one important element. But another, equally (if not more) important factor, is for the disciple-maker to *demonstrate the principles and truths in action.*

○ Your behavior matters! Much of what children do is imitating people they trust and respect. That is why parents still matter these days, even though parents spend less time with their children than has historically been the case. Again, the relational factor is huge, but so is how you show what the Jesus life looks like in real time.

○ Most pastors, parents, and churches claim to do an excellent or very good job at discipling people. The evidence suggests otherwise. And that's why *a measurement and accountability process* is so important. Trying hard is not enough. Feeling good about your efforts is insufficient. Assuming that your points got through is inadequate. The more you can incorporate objective assessments into your discipling journey, the more effective you will be.

○ More often than not, the process will be qualitative rather than quantitative. It is not necessary to generate statistical measures to prove you're making a difference; you need a constant flow of reliable, unbiased information that persuasively shows the protégé is becoming more like Jesus.

• **Prepared for the transition.** You will eventually reach a point in the relationship where you have done what you can to help your disciple-in-training become more like Jesus. The process will not be complete. Each of us is always on the journey of learning how to be better imitators of Jesus; we are never fully spiritually mature, never wholly Christlike.

Years ago, a management consultant wrote a mega-selling book that offered one simple but profound thought: Corporations show their approval of employee performance by promoting people to positions they are incapable of mastering. He described that as reaching their level of incompetence. That's what we're seeking as a disciple-maker: to reach the point where we have done everything we can to help a protégé catch up to us. At that point—your point of spiritual incompetence, which we all have—it will be time for you to step aside so the newly-minted disciple can continue to grow. And hopefully you can continue to learn new facets of discipleship from whoever is mentoring you.

BE CAREFUL—AND HONEST

For the record, if you are not sold out to Jesus Christ, do not try to pass yourself off as a disciple and then compound that mistake by trying to get other people, especially a child, to aspire to your spiritual condition. Face it, you cannot give what you do not have.

The research clearly shows that *most parents* of children in America are not disciples of Jesus, even though most parents describe themselves as Christian.[51] Much as some parents want to take primary responsibility for the spiritual development of their children, they will not grow their children to be Christlike if they themselves do not bear His imprint on their heart, mind, and soul. They will reproduce who they are.

Even more disturbing is that my research also reveals that *most pastors* of Christian churches in America—including most pastors leading the ministries to children—are not genuine disciples of Jesus.[52] Why is the church in America shrinking? Why are there fewer and fewer real followers of Jesus populating the United States? Even though most of the religious professionals who hold the disciple-making positions are not disciples, we fool ourselves into thinking that extensive education and ecclesiastical titles qualify those who hold them to be our chief disciple-makers. Shame on us. As Galatians 6:5 warns us, you can only reap what you sow.

If you want to be a disciple of Jesus but are not much different in spiritual maturity than your child, please do not try to pass yourself off as a disciple-maker. Do whatever is needed to connect your child with a genuine, spiritually mature disciple of Christ who is enthusiastic about discipling him. Or find someone who is a passionate and more advanced follower of Jesus and come under their wing yourself. By placing yourself under the guidance of a mentor, you will model what you are asking your child to do at the same time that you benefit from being raised up to be a spiritual champion.

On the other hand, if you are truly a disciple of the Lord, please obey His command that you make disciples. If you have a biblical worldview and are skilled at translating biblical truth into a biblical lifestyle, you are a precious resource sent to help others grow in obedience and service to Christ.

The only way you will be spiritually fulfilled is by satisfying the Great Commission. The only way America can be restored is by our existing disciples reproducing themselves spiritually, making new disciples. Make the commitment and follow the insights discovered about how best to invest in those who can become disciples. In the following chapters, we will look more closely at the substance of that process.

Jesus took twelve ordinary guys and turned them into an incredible band of disciple-makers. They were unlikely candidates for such success. Surely you can match their performance if you put your mind and heart into it.

05

DISCIPLE-MAKING PRACTICE #2 *EMBRACE BIBLICAL TRUTH PRINCIPLES*

nce a child is willing to pursue the life of a disciple, understanding what a disciple is, and having the necessary relationship in place with a competent and committed discipler, it's time to move aggressively to strategically develop the belief system of the child. Beliefs are of paramount importance because they determine how a person will live.

"You do what you believe" is a simple reminder that nobody wants to live in a state of cognitive dissonance, where you wrestle with internal conflicts caused by your competing beliefs, or by tensions between your core beliefs and your lifestyle choices. All of that "spiritual noise" creates anxiety and confusion. Your faith should be a source of strength and clarity, not chaos and angst.

For a disciple, the ultimate objective is not simply to harmonize belief and behavior for the sake of inner peace. It is to learn and appropriate the beliefs of Jesus so that your resulting actions reflect the ways of the Lord. Or, more succinctly, the goal is to think like Jesus so you can live like Jesus.

Biblically speaking, discipling a child is meant to be done by the child's parents. They need not undertake that journey in a vacuum, though. The community of faith to which the parents are connected is expected to provide practical support for the parents in that disciple-making effort. The child's family is designed to be the primary implementer of spiritual development while receiving ongoing assistance from the church family.

Unfortunately, if you study how children in Christian homes are raised these days, you discover that they are exposed to biblical truths and principles randomly and irregularly. The child's worldview continues to develop because it is a need that must be met in order to make decisions throughout the day.

Sadly, because parents and other authority figures are not intentionally and strategically working to build the child's worldview to primarily reflect biblical truths, the child's worldview develops by default. The resulting worldview is syncretism.

HOW WORLDVIEW DEVELOPS

A person's worldview is a combination of trial-and-error decisions (i.e., lessons based on experiences), reason-based choices, emotional preferences, and beliefs based on trust. It seems unlikely that we will ever know what proportion of a person's worldview developed from each of those distinctive stimuli. But we know that there are particular life elements that an individual must come to grips with in order to make sense of life and move forward each day. Those elements—which form the substance of a worldview—relate to many perspectives, including the following concepts:

- The purpose of life

- The existence, source(s), and implications of truth

- Moral judgment and personal applications

- The existence of a supernatural dimension and supernatural forces or beings

- Spiritual practices

- The contours, purposes, and role of family
- How the universe and life began and is sustained
- The value of human life
- How history influences the present and future
- Human nature and individual character
- Lifestyle options and merit
- Interpersonal relationships
- Basis of behavioral judgment
- Eternal destiny
- Spiritual relationships

With each passing day, a child collects more information about how life works, his/her place in the world, where they are headed in life, and how to optimize their experience on Earth. While there are numerous individuals and organizations that seek to influence their decisions in this regard, the absence of a standardized or generally accepted philosophy of life leads the child to believe that worldview is a customized process; they must make their own choices, just as other people have made theirs.

Recognizing that each child incrementally constructs their worldview according to their accumulated experiences, knowledge, feelings, and relationships, those who hope to provide guidance in that process might consider several facets borne out by our research before attempting to influence the child's worldview.

AN EXPERIMENTAL PROCESS

Making sense of life is not easy. There are constant cues and lessons, but absorbing them in a way that forms a pathway to understanding and satisfaction is difficult. Even when a trusted authority figure models godly beliefs and behaviors, and capably explains how to embody that worldview, young people usually test what is offered and tinker with it. They retain the perspectives they like and discard those they do not.

In cases where they are uncertain whether an element of a proposed worldview is one they want to adopt, they continue to experiment until they reach a satisfying conclusion. In that sense, worldview development is an art, not science.

IMITATING THEIR PARENTS

For millions of young children, their parents are trusted advisers. However, one of the more intriguing outcomes from my recent research is that surprisingly few children these days accept worldview teaching from their parents without question. The reason is that when an authority figure, such as a mother or father, offers a life principle to their child, the youngster then considers whether their parent follows their own advice.

The research noted that because parents sometimes teach one thing but live another, their child is likely to conclude that their parent is just as confused and searching as they are. They remain open to trying out the practical suggestions and worldview principles provided by their parents, but due to the inconsistency between *talk* and *walk*, children are prone to perceiving parental advice to be an option to consider rather than truth to accept.

WORLDVIEW IS A BIG ISSUE TO TACKLE

Wayne Grudem, one of America's preeminent theologians, kidded me about worldview, noting that to have a completely biblical worldview, a person would have to know everything in the Bible, believe it all, and follow it without fault. Given that we are all sinners from birth, that's an impossible challenge. The point is that our version of a biblical worldview does not mean we have achieved spiritual perfection; it simply enables us to be more like Christ—not Christ, but more like Him than would be the case if we did not embrace a substantial number of His beliefs and a deep desire to put those beliefs into practice.

But no matter how deeply motivated we are to be like Jesus, accepting and applying biblical principles is a big assignment. One way of accomplishing the task is by following the advice embedded in the old joke about eating an elephant. Knowing that the average elephant weighs about 10,000 pounds, how do you eat an elephant? One bite at a time.

Developing a biblical worldview can be treated the same way. How can we learn, believe, and practice biblical truth when the Bible is hundreds and hundreds of pages and contains hundreds of principles for life? One principle at a time. And to facilitate gleaning the wisdom of each principle and placing it in a memorable and credible context, we might allocate those principles to categories.

In fact, upon investigating the worldview curriculum used at Arizona Christian University (where I do research and teach, known as a premier biblical worldview university), it became apparent that the principles shared fall into eight modules of wisdom. These modules cover the following areas:

- Bible, Truth, and Morals
- Faith Practices
- Family and the Value of Life
- God, Creation, and History
- Human Character and Human Nature
- Lifestyle, Behavior, and Interpersonal Relationships
- Purpose and Calling
- Sin, Salvation, and Relationship with God

Each of these categories addresses critical subject matter. When blended into a comprehensive philosophy of life, these truths, principles, and commands enable us to make decisions that comply with God's expectations. They are not the only way to organize His truth in a manner that facilitates recall and deployment, but they are a useful tool for simplifying what might otherwise seem like an overwhelming or even impossible task.

THE COMPETITION FOR WORLDVIEW SUPREMACY

To compound the magnitude of the worldview development challenge, we must understand that the biblical worldview is not the sole worldview from which children can choose—or to which they are frequently exposed. There are well over a dozen comprehensive systems of thought and practice that constitute worldviews to choose from. Some of the best-known (and most popular) among those are listed and briefly described below.

- **Biblical Theism.** This is the theological name for the biblical worldview. This perspective begins with accepting the existence and sovereignty of God and His words as contained in the Bible and contends that those words were provided by God for His creation (people) to flourish while on Earth and to understand the pathway to peace and eternity with Him.

    In this system of thinking, human life is sacred, family is the primary institution through which humanity grows and thrives, our lives are designed to relate to our perfect and just Creator through a transforming relationship with Jesus Christ, and life is optimized when we are consistently obedient to God. We engage with both God and humanity to express and experience love, peace, and joy.

- **Eastern Mysticism.** Buddhism and Hinduism are the most common expressions of this interpretation of reality, providing an alternative to Western philosophy and lifestyle.

Americans are most familiar with this worldview through a cultural adaptation often described as New Age. Eastern Mysticism and its variants teach that there is no personal God, but there are powerful life forces that form the cosmos, of which we are all part, and through which we are all interrelated and interdependent. This view not only rejects the Christian notion of a personal, holy, and active God but also dismisses absolute moral truth and human reasoning as ways of understanding and responding appropriately to reality.

Adherents of this view teach that, as part of the universal consciousness and continuity in which everything is part of an eternal, impersonal life force, the ultimate purpose and goal of life is to transcend the material world to reach a unified spiritual expression.

• **Marxism.** Named after German philosopher Karl Marx, this point of view contends that life is all about handling the inevitable oppression, especially economic and political, that people will face on Earth.

Marxism vehemently rejects organized religion, which it infamously labels the "opiate of the people." And it rejects the Bible, the existence of God, life after death, the innate value of human life, and moral absolutes.

Further, it sees no value in family, marriage, individuality, tradition, and individual ownership of property. Its solution to the hardships of life is to empower cultural elites to apply their superior intellect and character to lead humanity forward and make life tolerable.

Like many worldviews, Marxism has offshoots that emphasize and apply various elements to the exclusion or minimizing of other elements. Among the best-known variants of Marxism are Critical Race Theory, Socialism, and Communism.

- **Moralistic Therapeutic Deism.** This is a relatively recent addition to the worldview parade, emerging as a popular but fake form of biblical Christianity within the past three decades. Among the chief tenets of MTD are believing that God exists but is not involved in people's lives; people can earn their salvation by being good; the ultimate purpose of life is to be happy (experienced by feeling good about oneself and being good to others); absolute moral truths do not exist; and the Bible is a useful but flawed and unreliable guidebook from which you must carefully pick and choose what principles are valid.

  Do not be fooled; this popular version of counterfeit Christianity is upbeat and hopeful, but it puts mankind at the center of a meaningful life, rather than God.

- **Nihilism.** Popularized by another German philosopher, Friedrich Nietzsche, this perspective dismisses the supernatural, moral absolutes, ethical norms, and political and social institutions. Nihilism argues that life is pointless and random and therefore has no meaning, purpose, truth, or value. It goes so far as to say that knowledge and meaning do not exist; they are mere illusions. Because nothing matters and there is no higher organism (e.g., God) to whom we answer, life is justifiably self-indulgent, but inevitably produces extreme pessimism and skepticism. (In fact, Nihilists are reported to have the highest suicide rate, which is philosophically consistent with their vision of life.)

- **Postmodernism.** Initially conceived as a response to Marxism, which Postmodern thinkers vehemently rejected, Postmodernism repudiates all large-scale explanations of our existence and progress (which they call metanarratives, such as Christianity).

  Postmodernism rejects the idea of absolute truth; views material success as the only meaningful outcome of human life; and is known for rejecting all forms of human organization and theory (referred to as deconstructionism) without providing alternatives.

- **Secular Humanism.** This worldview places science and human reason on a pedestal. With mankind at the center of all things, Secular Humanism denies the existence of God, Jesus, or other supernatural beings; is the primary advocate of evolution; and describes human beings as biological machines.

  The environmental movement is an outgrowth of this philosophy since they believe that nature is the most powerful force in existence and must be actively protected. In this way of life, science, reason, and experience determine what can be identified as moral and ethical behavior. Because this life is all there is, this wholly individualistic philosophy identifies meaning and success as the pursuit of personal happiness and social justice.

Our research finds that although most Americans cannot describe the substance of any of these worldviews with any clarity or comprehensiveness, most of us have latched on to a few elements in each of these worldviews. And, as you will see in chapter 9, the media we pay attention to is constantly assaulting us with ideas drawn from all these ways of describing life.

SYNCRETISM HAS THE EDGE

Children are exposed to ideas from all these worldviews, without realizing the roots of those ideas. And because there is usually no person or entity involved in the child's life that is coaching the child in the development of their worldview, it forms organically. The name given to the most common worldview in America, then, is syncretism, which refers to the combining of philosophical ideas appropriated from a variety of worldviews and developed into a customized understanding of life.

In the United States in 2023, just 4% of adults—and 2% of the parents of children under the age of thirteen—possessed a biblical worldview. In stark contrast, 94% of adults had a syncretistic worldview.[53] These statistics shock many people, especially since a majority of adults claim that they have a biblical worldview.[54] Tracking studies of worldview, however, suggest otherwise. In fact, even among individuals who can be classified as "born-again Christians"—that is, people who believe that when they die, they will live eternally in the presence of God but only because they have confessed their sins and accepted Jesus Christ as their Savior—a mere one out of every eight (13%) has a biblical worldview while more than four out of five of them (86%) are practicing syncretists.[55]

By definition, syncretism is the blending of views from two or more of the comprehensive worldview systems. In reality, that blend is typically a patchwork of conflicting and sometimes irreconcilable beliefs and values used to navigate life. Almost all people who are practitioners of syncretism hold beliefs that are contradictory, or practice behaviors that are inconsistent with what they claim to believe.

This brings to mind the apostle Paul's self-indictment written to the Romans, "I want to do what is right, but I can't. I want to do what is good, but I don't. I don't want to do what is wrong, but I do it anyway."[56] Paul describes the power of sin working in Him as the culprit responsible for his undesired thoughts and actions. Embracing syncretism—even unconsciously—is a pathway to leading a sin-plagued life.

You may never have heard of syncretism, but it is nothing new; it has been a thorn in the side of humans and the Christian faith for centuries. Paul, Peter, and others scolded their contemporaries for mixing popular ideas with biblical principles, just as Jesus criticized the Sadducees and Pharisees (the Jewish leaders of His day) for merging biblical truths with cultural preferences. Unfortunately, pagan Christianity has been more common throughout church history than a pure form of Jesus's faith.[57]

Many people whose dominant worldview is syncretism also embrace some elements of biblical thinking. The problem is not so much that they completely reject what the Bible teaches, but that they do not adopt most of the life principles presented in God's Word—and because so many of them consider themselves to be Christian, they are unaware of the problem.

CHALLENGES FOR THE BIBLICAL WORLDVIEW

Why do most Americans lack a coherent worldview? One important reason is that Americans are not directly taught about worldview as part of their education. That's why most people's worldview develops by default.

People incorporate beliefs and behaviors that reflect the culture around them. We see this in messages delivered in arts and entertainment, comments made on social media platforms, themes delivered through news reports, political statements made by public leaders, principles derived from laws and public policies, and ideas and expectations absorbed from conversations and experiences with other people. Having no formal or systematic training in worldview, we are prone to accept philosophical concepts that feel comfortable, are convenient or popular, or are modeled by people we trust.

Past studies conducted among churchgoing adults have found that biblical information offered in churches and ministry settings is more likely to be treated as historical ideas to be considered than lifestyle principles to be accepted and applied. One of my research projects revealed that sermons that provide good biblical information often fail to change lives because that presentation is disconnected from a consistent and comprehensive body of principles designed for life application.

That information is like the dots on a paint-by-number sheet that has no numbers next to any of the dots to indicate how to connect the dots and form a useful picture. In other words, when it comes to worldview development, Christians have stored up lots of information but have no idea what to do with that body of knowledge.

Unfortunately, that is what parents, Christian schools, churches, and Christian media are doing with our children. We pride ourselves on giving them scriptural truths and principles but overlook their inability to convert those insights into a philosophy that will result in a Bible-driven life.

WORLDVIEW WAKE-UP CALL: TEENAGE REALITY

As we did in chapter 2, when we evaluated how well ministry to children is doing based on the condition of newly-minted teenagers, let's again consider how we're doing with the worldview development of children by returning to early teens.

Using the same assessment process we use among adults, the Cultural Research Center worldview survey of teenagers shows that we are in crisis mode. *Currently, less than 1% of early-teens have a biblical worldview, with only 5% even close to having such a perspective. The prevailing worldview among 99% of young teens is syncretism.*

If there is any encouragement to be gained from the data related to teenagers, less than one-half of one percent of them is strongly connected to any of the primary competing worldviews that we measure (Eastern Mysticism, Marxism, Moralistic Therapeutic Deism, Nihilism, Postmodernism, and Secular Humanism).

But a reality check emerges upon exploring how young teens are doing in relation to the worldview modules described above. Specifically, there is not a single content module for which even one out of every twenty young teens consistently embraces biblical views. In other words, there are not just one or two areas in which the worldview of young teens is radically deficient; teenagers are sorely lacking in biblical belief across the board.

THE 7 CORNERSTONES—A LIFE PRESERVER

One of the most common questions I get from parents and other influencers is where to start and how to proceed in helping children (or other people, as well) to develop a biblical worldview.

Fortunately, deeper dives into the data have discovered what we refer to as "the seven cornerstones of a biblical worldview."[58] According to the research, these are seven particular beliefs without which a person is very unlikely to develop a consistently biblical life of thought and action. More than four out of five adults (83%)

who embrace these seven basic biblical teachings possess a biblical worldview. In comparison, only a relative handful of people who do not believe the seven foundations (2%) hold a biblical worldview.[59]

Obviously, very few people are able to overcome the influence of the competing worldview perspectives we considered earlier in the chapter unless they embrace *all seven* of the biblical cornerstone principles. One's response to the seven cornerstones essentially determines one's ability and likelihood of developing a biblical mind and lifestyle.

These seven precepts are like a foundation on which any child can build a purposeful and influential life that glorifies God. Starting with these simple and basic biblical tenets empowers a child to construct a spiritual base that is scripturally solid, leading to life choices that are not only consistent and defensible, but also fulfilling and comforting.

These guidelines are powerful and transformative. Knowing these truths and applying them every day provides a child with the strength and confidence needed to make solid decisions every time, no matter how turbulent and challenging our culture becomes.

Timeless truths, consistently applied, produce a life of righteousness, goodness, peace, joy, and influence. That's exactly what a biblical worldview is meant to deliver: not just a philosophy of life that is biblical for its own sake, but one that enables its bearer to consistently think and live like Jesus.

What beliefs are necessary to have a strong foundation for a biblical worldview? You might be surprised that the required beliefs are basic Christian teachings, not advanced or sophisticated theological constructs. In fact, many of these principles and commands are taught to children who attend Sunday school, Christian schools, or have devout Christian parents. In the next chapter we'll discuss why so many of these children do not embrace these teachings as the foundation of their worldview.

These worldview cornerstones are deceptively simple. Being defined by them requires more than casual assent. For these to become personal foundations for life, a child must both understand the principles and harbor a passionate, thoughtful ownership of those beliefs in order to translate them into consistent obedience.

CORNERSTONE #1

There is one supreme being as revealed by the orthodox, biblical understanding of God.

A basic understanding of the existence and nature of God is a crucial building block for a biblical worldview. Many worldviews (like Marxism, Nihilism, Postmodernism, and Secular Humanism, among others) do not believe in the existence of a supreme being. Christianity is one of the faiths that does, but the marketplace of ideas in our country bombards our children with many divergent gods and characteristics of deities that do not square with biblical teachings.

What distinguishes the God of Israel from other alleged deities? The Bible identifies some of His attributes as being the Creator of all things; the sustainer of humankind and the universe; omnipotent;

omniscient; omnipresent; loving; just; merciful; and relational. He is a unique presence who wants us to thrive, and He makes provisions for that outcome.

He created humanity to be in relationship with Him and to focus our life on engaging with, serving, and ultimately answering to Him. He is involved in the affairs of mankind. Our eternal destiny is in His hands.

CORNERSTONE #2

All human beings are sinful by nature; the sin nature has moral considerations and consequences.

The biblical narrative explains that every person begins life with a sinful nature inherited from Adam (sometimes called "original sin") and that the temptation to sin is always present in our lives. The narrative also notes that God provides people with power delivered through His Holy Spirit to give us the authority and will to deny the lure of sin in favor of righteous choices that honor God.

Each day we make hundreds of decisions; every one of them is an opportunity to demonstrate our commitment to being like Jesus. Every choice we make either pleases or displeases God. No human being lives a sin-free life or consistently makes God-honoring choices. Regardless of our intentions, we are all guilty of sin and are incapable of eliminating that tendency through our own actions or power.

CORNERSTONE #3

The consequences of our sin can only be forgiven and eliminated through Jesus Christ. This forgiveness is available only through our personal, sincere acknowledgment and confession of our sins and complete reliance on His grace for the forgiveness of those sins.

Every human being sins and is therefore incapable of earning God's favor based on merit. As the apostle Paul explained the situation, every human sins and thereby falls short of God's standards,[60] leaving us separated from Him.

But as our loving Creator, God made a way out of our sin dilemma by sending Jesus Christ to take on the sins of the human race and to die as a substitutionary sacrifice on our behalf. Through that act, every person has access to forgiveness and becomes righteous in God's eyes.

But this is not an automatic, universal provision of grace. It requires our admission of sin and prayer for Jesus's forgiveness, and true repentance (a commitment to not repeating the sin).

Our contrition before the Savior is the only means for gaining righteousness in God's eyes. Through Him we may receive eternal salvation, but it is a gift of grace, love, mercy, and compassion. Absent that gift, we remain condemned and hopeless. Thanks to that gift, we have hope and a pathway to glory.

CORNERSTONE #4

The entire Bible is true, reliable, and relevant, making it the best moral guide for every person, in all situations.

God wants us to flourish on Earth. To help us experience that victory, He gave us a blueprint for life: the Bible. Millions of Americans think of the Bible as a book describing an angry God who punishes people for their wrongdoing and is packed with behavioral limitations and warnings.

However, a more accurate view is to see the Bible as a book of hope, encouragement, life principles, and practical lessons. The stories, commands, principles, warnings, and wisdom in the Bible point us to a better life outcome by doing things His way.

And because God is the embodiment of love and truth, following those words lead us to a moral life in ways that human emotion and reason cannot. People who follow His principles and commands experience victory through their faithful obedience. Those who resist and reject the Scriptures in favor of accommodating their emotions or societal norms and preferences, pay the price for their ignorance and arrogance.

CORNERSTONE #5

Absolute moral truths exists—and those truths are defined by God, described in the Bible, and are unchanging across time and cultures.

Moral truth is the delineation of right and wrong. Absolute moral truth says that there are determinations of right and wrong that are independent of the individual's emotions, circumstances, or preferences. Moral truths exist whether or not we acknowledge them, like them, understand them, or apply them. The consequences of obeying or disobeying those absolutes vary, but the absolutes themselves do not change. In a world characterized by chaos, absolute moral truths are an aberration because they are completely predictable.

However, that predictability does not mean they are always obvious. The only sure way of identifying moral absolutes is by consulting the inerrant source of truth, and the ultimate source of inerrant truth is the God of Israel. He *is* truth. He cannot lie or deceive because that is against His nature and purposes.

And because truth is central to His prized creation (human beings) experiencing a good life on Earth, He has provided an explanation of truth for us, words designed to enable us to thrive. Those words are the Bible. Those moral absolutes are made accessible to us through descriptions provided in various forms—principles, stories, warnings, and commands.

Truth, when properly understood and fully applied, leads to righteousness, which pleases God and empowers us to know, love, and serve Him better. Circumstances, emotions, norms, desires, and preferences change over time; truth does not. It is a fixed, reliable standard that is the same in all ages, in all places, for all people. You cannot know absolute truth by following the culture or your feelings; it is only available through the Scriptures.

CORNERSTONE #6

The ultimate purpose of human life is to know, love, and serve God with all your heart, mind, strength, and soul.

Jesus was clear in telling people that the most important of the commandments is that we love God with all our heart, soul, mind, and strength.[61] In His mind, there is nothing more important than that commitment. To genuinely love Him, we must know Him—and knowing everything we can about God produces a humbling, profound love for Him. That love, in turn, generates a deep desire to pursue everything we are capable of doing, in service to Him and His purposes.

Satan works hard to distract or prevent us from investing in that relationship. But human fulfillment and joy cannot be experienced until we clarify our true life's purpose and wholeheartedly devote ourselves to fulfilling that commitment.

CORNERSTONE #7

Success on Earth is best understood as consistent obedience to God—in thoughts, words, and actions.

If the purpose of a person's life is to love God in every conceivable way, focusing on His truths, applying those principles every moment and in every situation, effectively worshiping and serving Him at all times, then obedience to His principles makes us "successful" here on Earth.

This is a difficult truth for millions of Americans to adopt because it renders the pursuits and outcomes that the world promotes—wealth, fame, achievement, power, sexual fulfillment, knowledge, prestige, happiness, comfort—to be unrelated to real success. The Creator alone determines the criteria for the success of those whom He creates. Jesus plainly stated that we will be His disciples when we obey His teachings.[62] That succinctly defines the parameters of human success.

STATE OF THE CORNERSTONES

Many people have suggested to me that they have already taught their children the cornerstone principles, so they are expecting their young ones to develop a biblical worldview. But it may not be as clear-cut as those adults believe. Simply hearing a teaching or even parroting it back to their mentor does not mean a person believes it. You know when someone believes it when they act upon it.

Maybe the best example of the difference between exposure to information and believing that information is Satan's demons.[63] James describes them as having knowledge about God but acting in opposition to it. If they really believed in the goodness and power of God, wouldn't they serve Him instead of Satan? Translated into life today, in this era of "fake news," you have probably been exposed to information that was alleged to be true, but you did not accept its veracity enough to act upon it.

That is why James wrote, "Don't just listen to God's word. You must do what it says. Otherwise, you are only fooling yourselves."[64]

You do what you believe; you do not always apply things that you have heard. The advertising world lives and dies on the concept of repetition. Based upon research, a person must have multiple exposures to a message before it is likely to persuade them to accept the information as sufficiently accurate and meaningful enough to act upon it as prescribed.

If you are mentoring someone, it is not enough to teach them a lesson and walk away, convinced that your job is done. Observe how a child responds to a truth principle that you have shared with them. If they continue to live in opposition or indifference to it, seek additional opportunities to understand the point of disconnection and to express that biblical principle in a different manner.

Remember, demonstrating its application through your personal behavior is a powerful endorsement of a concept.

CONVEYING THE CORNERSTONES

Thankfully, our survey with a national sample of adolescents—defined as children eight- to twelve-years-old—provides a first-hand, objective look at where young Americans stand in relation to the seven cornerstones of a biblical worldview.

Overall, we can track the progression of development in their awareness of and belief in the cornerstones by age. The survey did not find *any* children eight or nine years old who had biblical beliefs for all seven cornerstones. Adopting all seven cornerstones first occurred among children at ages ten (3%) and eleven (4%) and then doubled to 8% at age twelve.

Most young people believe some of the cornerstone principles by age eight. Only about one-third of eight-year-olds (37%) did not accept any of the cornerstones. That proportion declined to about one-quarter of children in the nine-to-eleven age bracket, and dropped to just one out of every seven children (14%) of age twelve who do not believe in any of the seven cornerstone teachings.

These seven perspectives have some "stickiness" in the minds and hearts of children, but clearly more intentional efforts are necessary to propel them to a biblical worldview. A look at how many adolescents believe each of the cornerstone teachings offers insight into which of those are most challenging for children to accept.

Cornerstone #1: There is one supreme being as revealed by the orthodox, biblical understanding of God.

Two out of every three eight-to-ten-year-olds (65%) possess a biblical understanding of the God of Israel. That number rises to three out of four (74%) among eleven- and twelve-year-olds.

Cornerstone #2: All human beings are sinful by nature; this sin nature has moral considerations and consequences.

One-third of adolescents (35%) have this point of view, topping out at 42% among eleven- and twelve-year-olds.

Cornerstone #3: The consequences of our sin can only be forgiven and eliminated through Jesus Christ. That forgiveness is available only through our personal, sincere

acknowledgment and confession of our sins and complete reliance on His grace for the forgiveness of those sins.

This is the aspect of belief reflecting the greatest growth during the adolescent years. Just one-quarter of the younger segment (i.e., ages eight, nine, and ten) endorse this cornerstone, compared to nearly twice as many (49%) among those who are in the older age segment (i.e., eleven and twelve years old).

Cornerstone #4: The entire Bible is true, reliable, and relevant, making it the best moral guide for every person, in all situations.

Overall, one-fourth of adolescents believe the Bible provides us a description of moral truth. The proportion rises from two out of ten in the younger niche (20%) to three out of ten in the older group (31%).

Cornerstone #5: Absolute moral truth exists—and those truths are defined by God, described in the Bible, and are unchanging across time and cultures.

Just one out of every five adolescents believes that absolute moral truth exists. There is positive growth in that perspective as children age, increasing from 17% among the eight-to-ten-year-olds up to 27% among the eleven- and twelve-year-olds.

Cornerstone #6: The ultimate purpose of human life is to know, love, and serve God with all your heart, mind, strength, and soul.

In total, one-quarter of adolescents believe in the life purpose defined in Scripture. However, that proportion jumps from 25% among younger children to 43% among the older adolescents.

Cornerstone #7: Success on Earth is best understood as consistent obedience to God—in thoughts, words, and actions.

One out of every six children (17%) agrees that success is about consistent obedience to God, with little change across the adolescent years.

Generally speaking, we are making too little headway in helping children understand the biblical views of truth, purpose, and success. We have made somewhat more headway regarding the sinfulness of mankind and the need for Jesus to save us from our sins, but even in that regard—which gets a lot of attention in church programs geared to adolescents—most young people head into their teen years without a biblical perspective on those matters. Truly, it is only in relation to their concept of God that a substantial proportion of adolescents reflect the Bible's view.

Before we move on, consider the worldview data among teenagers in relation to these outcomes among adolescents. We know that embracing the seven cornerstones usually leads to a person developing a biblical worldview. Among the eleven- and twelve-year-olds interviewed, 6% believe in all seven of the cornerstone principles. Yet when we look at teenagers, less than 1% has a biblical worldview. How can that be?

The spiritual explanation for this pattern could be Jesus's teaching, known as "the parable of the four soils."[65] In that lesson, Jesus explained to His disciples that even though good seed may be sown (i.e., good biblical teaching to those who are listening), the seed often fails to produce the expected yield.

When His disciples failed to understand the analogy that He used concerning the planting of seeds and the development of a person's worldview, He explained the meaning. Some hearers either don't understand or do not quite accept the lesson, so Satan distracts them from working through it or offers them a competing point of view that is more appealing.

Others hear the message and give it some consideration but abandon that belief once things get tough; they choose an alternative perspective that gives them greater or more immediate benefit. Another segment become distracted by the worries and snares of daily life, fixating on gaining the riches of the world rather than surrendering all to focus on God and His call. There are relatively few, according to the Lord, who hear the teaching, believe it, act on it, and produce positive outcomes.

That may well be what happens during the transition from the adolescent to teenage years. By the time children reach seventeen or eighteen years of age, less than half as many believe the biblical description of God as was the case at ages eleven and twelve—a serious and game-changing decline in progress. In fact, a comparison of the beliefs of the oldest adolescents and the oldest teenagers also shows a severe decline in the acceptance of the cornerstone teachings related to five of the other six factors: the sinfulness of humans, the need for Jesus to save us from our sins, the reliability of Scripture, purpose as full devotion to God, and defining success as consistent obedience to God.

The only cornerstone which does not show evidence of serious degradation over the teen years is perspectives on the Bible: That showed virtually no change from ages eleven through eighteen, with only one-third accepting the Bible as being the true and reliable words of God to humanity.

Hit-and-run discipleship—the process where we deliver the necessary information, check that box off on our discipling list, then move on to the next obligation without ensuring that the first effort has taken root and borne fruit—does not work. If you want to disciple a child, realize that transformational impact comes from a strategic, consistent, long-term, relational investment that ensures biblical truth is heard, understood, embraced, and applied.

A FULL BIBLICAL WORLDVIEW

Laying a strong foundation through the adoption of the seven cornerstones is a terrific start, but it is not the entire effort required to help young people develop a genuinely biblical worldview.

Remember, just 3% of all adults incorporate the seven cornerstones into their life.

And among that small segment of the population that has adopted the seven cornerstones as part of their philosophy of life, one out of every six of them never complete the task—that is, they fail to do the rest of the work necessary to embrace consistently biblical thinking and behavior and thus become a genuine disciple of Jesus.

What are they missing? What else should children be taught and held accountable for as they move through their most impressionable, worldview-forming years? Here are some of the things that we measure in the eight modules of belief and behavior for you to consider.[66]

Since a biblical worldview insinuates encompassing every biblical thought and its corollary actions into one's worldview, we would have to reproduce most of the Bible to cover the full gamut of principles and commands. But the following is at least an extensive and viable, albeit not comprehensive, list of the elements to involve in the development process.

Note that most of these elements are associated with two or more biblical principles or commands and are therefore more robust than this skeletal listing suggests.

- Nature of moral truth (e.g., subjective, absolute, conditional, biblically-defined, etc.)

- Origin and basis of truth

- Reliability and authority of the Bible

- Optimal source of moral guidance
- Morality of spreading false information (i.e., gossip)
- Morality of having an abortion
- Morality of sexual relations among unmarried people
- Morality of intentional deceit (i.e., lying)
- Morality of suicide and euthanasia
- Beliefs about reincarnation
- Beliefs about life after death
- Basis of eternal judgment
- The "goodness" of humanity
- Role of Jesus Christ in individual salvation
- Definition and existence of sin
- Possibility of experiencing consistent intimacy with God
- Relationship of moral truth view and view of sin
- Engagement in consistent spiritual growth
- Sexual identity
- Belief in karma
- Practical definition of a successful life
- Sources of economic injustice
- Significance of faith in lifestyle
- Defining a legitimate marriage

- Perceived value of human life
- Universal purpose of life
- Willingness to try anything at least once
- Origins of the universe
- Meaning and significance of human history
- Supernatural aspects of creation
- Source of human life
- Extent of God's engagement in individual lives
- Existence and nature of a supreme being
- Divinity of Christ
- Existence and capacity of Satan
- Existence and capacity of the Holy Spirit
- Nature and continuity of the universe
- Commitment to practicing your faith
- Philosophy and practice of wealth management
- Personal responsibility to share the gospel
- Accepting Christianity as the one true faith
- Personal identification with Christianity
- Engagement in thanking and worshiping God
- Engagement in prayer
- Engagement in Bible study

- Engagement in repentance
- Engagement in a community of faith
- Engagement in serving people
- Existence of Heaven and Hell
- Eternal Destination

Don't get freaked out by the volume of entries on that list. If you study them carefully, you will realize that none of these elements exist in isolation; every biblical principle is connected to other biblical principles, making it easier to build a logical system of thought and action.

For instance, you will notice that there is a series of principles related to morality (e.g., moral choices concerning abortion, honesty, sexuality, and so forth). Each of those is connected to several other principles, such as the authority of the Bible, defining a legitimate marriage, the perceived value of human life, etc. God's philosophy of how we should live fits together like nuts in bolts if you take the time to associate the concepts with each other.

Eventually you will see the bigger picture formed by the intersection of these truths. At that point discussions about these factors, as well as the process of linking them together into a coherent worldview, becomes easier.

06
DISCIPLE-MAKING PRACTICE #3 *CONVERT BIBLICAL BELIEFS INTO ACTION*

eading a child to believe the right things is just part of the challenge of enabling a young person to become a disciple of Christ. An equally important undertaking is to promote the fledgling disciple fully, and passionately integrating those beliefs into a Christlike lifestyle.

When a burgeoning disciple translates principles into practices, she not only proves that she owns what she claims to believe; it also paves the way for her to spiritually reproduce herself, which is a crucial component of discipleship. After all, disciples are not born; they are coached into the life of Christ by other disciples, and generating more disciples is a fulfillment of the Great Commission (one of the commitments of practice #1, described in chapter 4).

This might sound to you like too much to expect from a child or perhaps too much pressure to place on their tiny shoulders. But don't underestimate their capacity and spiritual influence. Remember that peers are one of the primary influences on children. My research has highlighted the fact that many preteens who accept Jesus as their Savior do so because of the encouragement and follow-through of their friends.

In fact, the research even found that sometimes children lead their parents to Christ, or to a deeper spiritual commitment, by virtue of the sincerity and durability of their maturing faith. No wonder Jesus told His followers to not prevent children from coming to Him, and for pointing out to skeptical religious leaders that children were better at worshiping than they were.[67]

What can you do to help children translate biblical beliefs into biblical action? Here is what others are doing that has fostered that result.

ACTS OF OBEDIENCE TO GOD

Remember what we said about Jesus's requirements for being His disciple? Number one is to obey His teachings.

The logic trail for this requirement is simple. In order to obey, you have to know the rules. That's what practice #2 is all about, adopting biblical beliefs. Practice #3 is all about combining the spiritual truths we have adopted into appropriate action.

As a discipler, then, you must go beyond simply conveying biblical information to asking an important question regarding that information. That question is, "So what?"

Let's take the seven cornerstones as an example of how to guide a blossoming disciple.

Say you have been working with a child regarding the first cornerstone—believing that not only God exists, but that He is the omnipotent, omniscient, just, holy, perfect, and loving Creator of all things, and that He still rules and is involved in all He has created. The child has worked hard to understand what those attributes mean and how we know they are true. She indicates that after some initial confusion, followed by some doubts, she now wholeheartedly believes that such a deity exists and possesses those attributes.

So what?

At this point, we have the opportunity to think through the implications of the existence of God and to challenge the child to apply that belief to real-life situations. Here are a few of the implications of just one of those attributes: that God created the world and everything in it.

- The creator of something—at least one who retains control over the created entity—gets to determine the purpose and uses of that created entity. As I am part of His creation, God therefore retains the right and ability to call me to engage in certain situations of His choice for His own purposes. That means my life is not about what I feel like doing; it's up to me to work with Him to understand what He created me to do, and for me to do my best toward fulfilling that calling and purpose.

- The probability of my success in whatever He has called me to be and to do is exponentially increased if I can understand His vision for my existence and unique calling. If I jump into activity without grasping His larger vision and the special role He has ordained me to play within it, then I am likely to waste my limited resources and my personal potential and expend time and energy working at odds with Him.

- Because my biblical success depends on fitting into His plan, the more I can understand that plan, the more fulfillment I am likely to experience.

- As the Creator of my life and shaper of my experience, it is important to acknowledge and accept Him as the ultimate authority. He is in charge; I am not. I serve at His pleasure, for His pleasure. Just as He created me and has all authority over me and my future, so also He has the same authority over everything else He created (e.g., nature and humanity). My success, then, is dependent upon my submission to Him.

- The sheer magnitude and complexity of all that He created (and controls) is beyond my comprehension, much less my capacity. Therefore, knowing that He has a purpose and calling for me within the framework of His creation, when I struggle to accept, understand, or complete His assignment to me, then I can turn to Him for guidance, power, wisdom, and encouragement. Digging into the Scriptures shows that He promises to deliver these things to those who seek them through Him.

- As staggering as what He has created is, even my finite mind can recognize that His creation emerged from a purpose (to bring Him pleasure and glory), a plan (it is orderly, not random), unmatched creativity, and limitless capacity (power, intelligence, wisdom, imagination, and provision). As a being created in His image, I can learn from His process as I seek to carry out my purpose and calling.

- Human life must be important to Him, given scientific revelations that the conditions for life on Earth require very exact conditions that could not have happened randomly. Thus, while human existence remains seemingly precarious, it is apparently precious to Him. It should therefore be precious to me.

- God has given humans heightened intellect, which enables us to reason. In recognizing that I am made in His likeness yet not equal to Him in any regard, I must respect Him. Because every other person who exists is also created in His likeness, and they matter to Him, just as I do, I must respect them as well.

This is far from an exhaustive consideration of the implications of just one of the many attributes of God. We have not touched on any of the other factors incorporated into cornerstone #1—i.e., God is the ruler of all things and that He is just, perfect, loving, holy, involved, omnipotent, omniscient, and eternal. Each of those characteristics is vital to believe and understand—nor have we investigated using our "so what?" question.[68]

By the way, the expansive impact of those attributes is an example of why discipling someone is not a quick process. Taking the necessary time to not only teach a belief, but then to identify corollary actions, and explore the implications of the beliefs and actions requires an extended period of time with related experiences.

Disciples cannot be formed overnight. If instantaneous disciple-making were possible, Jesus might have spent less than three years investing in His twelve closest followers. If it took Him three years of concentrated and anointed effort, it would be foolish for us to think we have a better and faster way.

Perhaps the best way of helping an emergent disciple to apply the cornerstones is not by lecturing them on the facts but through reactions to the child's behaviors that relate to specific teachings. Using the Socratic approach to carry the conversation—i.e., asking questions concerning motive, action, response, and possibilities—you can dig into what took place and how well it squares with biblical beliefs and behavior.

MAKING IT REAL

A colleague described such a situation he encountered with his seven-year-old son. The young boy had been berating his younger sister, seeking to get back at her for derogatory comments she had made about his favorite baseball team. When the father and son were alone, the father confirmed what his son had done, then walked his son through a better process, never screaming at his son or lecturing him about the situation. He asked his son a logical series of questions that led the boy to a different conclusion about how to act—and why the alternative course of action was superior.

> *Dad:* David, do you remember when we were talking about how God made you and what that means about who you are?
>
> *Son:* Yes.
>
> *Dad:* Do you think God made your sister too?
>
> *Son:* Yes.
>
> *Dad:* But why do you believe God made her? Based on the names you called her, maybe the devil made her. What do you think?

Son: No, I think God made everyone, even her.

Dad: Okay, so if God made you, and He wants you to love and respect Him as your Creator and spiritual Father, and He made Rose, do you think He wants you to love and respect her too?

Son: I guess so.

Dad: People say all kinds of things about each other. Do you think the names we call each other can hurt someone, or make them feel bad, or maybe even suggest that they are not lovable?

Son: Yes. Sometimes people say things that hurt my feelings. Like Rose did.

Dad: I understand. Do you think calling her the names that you called her showed her you love her, and that you respect her, no matter what she said?

Son: No.

Dad: Do you think that the way you treated her showed God that you love Him and respect Him? Or that you are thankful that He gave you Rose as a sister?

Son: No.

Dad: Remind me, what were the names you called her that made her start crying and feeling bad?

Son: I called her stupid because she was saying dumb things about the Red Sox. And I said she was a creep, and I didn't want her to be my sister anymore because she was saying bad things. That was really mean of her. She wasn't respecting me or the Red Sox.

Dad: Do you remember the stories we read about Jesus and the men who were His followers? Do you remember we talked about how upsetting it must have been for Him to see them doing things that He had taught them were wrong?

Or how some of the things they said were wrong, and how Jesus must have been sad because they were not doing the things He was teaching them? Did He call them names, or tell them He would let bad things happen to them because they were not doing or saying the right things? What did He do?

Son: Jesus talked with them about what they did wrong and told them what they could do right. I guess He kept trying to show them He loved them by being their friend even though they did not listen to Him and were disappointing Him.

Dad: Good point, David. Did He yell at them or call them names, even though they let Him down?

Son: No, He just talked to them like normal.

Dad: That's true. You know, sometimes my friends, or Mommy, or even you and your sister say things that upset or hurt me. But I try to remember that God made you, He loves you, and He wants me to love you, and that if I do that, I am showing respect to Him.

Sometimes it's hard for me not to yell when people do something I asked them not to do. Their choices make me upset. But if I stop for a minute and think about the situation, I realize that yelling at them might make me feel better for a few moments, but it's not something that will make God happy.

Part of growing up is thinking about what Jesus would probably do if He were in your situation. If we figure that out, then we can try to do the same thing. And we talk about how Jesus tried to show that we are important to God and that He made us to love Him and serve Him. So we should respect other people the way He wants them to respect us, right?

Son: Yeah, I guess so. But what Rose said hurt my feelings.

Dad: Right, I understand that. Our words can hurt people, so we have to be very careful about what we say, all the time. When Rose called your favorite players bad and said the Red Sox will not win any more games, that made you angry and frustrated, didn't it? You were really disappointed in her.

Son: Yeah. But she likes the Orioles, and I didn't say mean things about them, even though they're worse than the Red Sox.

Dad: Well, that's good. But you did say mean things about her. Even though you were disappointed in her because of what she said, do you think what you said to her showed that you respect and love God, who created her and loves her? Or that it showed your love and respect for her?

Son: No.

Dad: What could you have said when she said mean things about your favorite team?

Son: I could have told her how good the Red Sox are, how they have a better record than the Orioles, and that last year the Orioles didn't even make the playoffs.

Dad: That's true. But is there anything you could have said that would show that you love her even when she says mean things, and that you respect her even when she disappoints you?

Son: Maybe I could have told her that what she said was wrong, that it hurt my feelings, and that I would not say the same things about her favorite team.

Dad: I like that, David. That would have been a better thing to say. I bet God would rather have you say things like that than to call your sister names that hurt her feelings and disrespect her. Do you think there's anything you can do now to make Rose feel better and to show her you love her?

Son: I can go hug her and tell her I'm sorry, and that she's not bad, and I shouldn't have said mean things to her. And that she shouldn't say mean things about the Red Sox.

My friend laughed and noted that the ending of their conversation wasn't perfect, but it was another step toward his son grasping the implications of God's character. I asked him how long it took to go through that dialogue with David. He said it was probably four or five minutes. When I pointed out that he is a busy guy and that exchange probably was not on his agenda for that morning—it was time he would never be able to reclaim—he smiled.

"I think that might have been the best five-minute investment of my day."

PRODUCING FRUIT

Jesus told His followers that true disciples produce spiritual fruit; that is another way in which we can help children translate their beliefs into action. Spiritual fruit begins with evidence of personal transformation. The most succinct statement of such internal fruit is in Galatians 5:22–23, where Paul notes that God generates fruit such as love, joy, peace, patience, kindness, goodness, faithfulness, gentleness, and self-control. Such fruit is born when we apply biblical beliefs in our life and change the way we think or respond to situations. This is allowing the Holy Spirit to alter our character.

Some simple and common religious expressions facilitate our spiritual transformation—yet most children do not participate in these ventures. Again, turning to the religious life of teenagers as an indication of what habits were bred in children before they "aged out," here is a profile of the basic religious activities that can set the stage for a life of discipleship.

- Taking time throughout each day to consciously and intentionally thank, praise, and worship God is a habit developed by true disciples. It places God at the center of our lives and deepens the intimacy we experience with Him.

  Sometimes we offer our focus and worship through a church service. More often, disciples enter God's presence through personal conversations with Him and expressing gratitude for who He is and how He guides us.

  When it comes to consciously and intentionally thanking, praising, and worshiping God outside of church services, only four out of every ten teens (40%) do so at least once a week.

- Personal communication with God through prayer is another way of reflecting spiritual fruit. Prayer is one of the primary means of expressing our deepest needs or emotions to God and one of the chief ways in which we ask Him to provide for us.

  Amazingly, less than half of all teenagers (45%) pray to God at least once a week.

- Reading or studying the Bible is the mark of someone committed to God's principles and commands. The Bible has been described as "God's love letter to His people," so taking the time to absorb His words not only guides us but reminds us of His unending love for us.

  Shockingly, outside of classes or church services, less than one-quarter of all teenagers (23%) commit any of their time to reading or studying the Bible during a typical week.

- If success is *consistent obedience to God*, then knowing and doing His will is a critical step toward achieving success in this world.

  Yet less than two out of five teens (38%) say they commit time and energy to knowing and doing God's will during a typical week.

- One of the great benefits of following Christ is knowing that He will forgive our sins—if we confess them and ask for His forgiveness. It's impossible to find a better offer than that, anywhere!

  Just one out of every three teenagers (36%) say they take advantage of God's grace by confessing their sins and seeking His forgiveness during a typical week.

- Attending religious services at a church used to be something that most children experienced each week. Times have certainly changed, as most young people no longer go to church often, and the frequency appears to diminish as a person gets older.

Unfortunately, only four out of every ten adolescents (40%) attend a church service in a typical week, and not quite three out of every ten teenagers (28%) attend a church service during a typical week.

- Turning to the Bible for guidance when making a moral choice is a natural habit developed by disciples. The Bible is the ultimate and only consistently valid determinant of how to act in a moral situation.

  Despite that, less than one out of every five teens (19%) use the Scriptures as their primary source of moral truth and guidance.

Each of those activities is fruitful in its own right. But a sign of moving from disparate religious activities to integrated disciple—that is, someone who not only embraces a full slate of biblical beliefs but also integrates those beliefs into an actively and consistently biblical lifestyle—is when such behaviors become habitual.

In other words, a child who is an integrated disciple is regularly and frequently praying, privately thanking and worshiping God, studying His words, devoting himself to knowing and doing God's will for his life, consistently identifying and confessing his sins, and asking for Jesus to forgive those transgressions.

That sounds like a pretty "normal" Christian life, doesn't it? Except that it's not. Among teenagers, only one out of every seven (14%) engage in all five of those simple, basic spiritual efforts in a typical week. If we add attending a church service, then it drops to one in ten teens (10%). And if we then eliminate the teens who essentially negate their Christian commitment by also regularly engaging in unbiblical endeavors—like chanting, repeating a New Age mantra, seeking guidance from a horoscope, or seeking revenge against anyone who harmed or offended them during the past week—the proportion plummets to only 4%.

So the challenge to a disciple-maker, then, is to not only help children embrace the seven cornerstone beliefs but to also participate in fundamental Christian practices such as those identified above. How can you do that?

Start by embodying those behaviors in your life and allowing the young ones to watch and learn. Children imitate the people they trust, so demonstrate good practices for them to mimic. Since you are a disciple, these should be normative in your spiritual regimen. Not only allowing your protégé to see you practicing your faith in these ways but also inviting them to participate alongside of you is a big deal.

Fortify that experience by pointing out Christian heroes who do these practices in the Scriptures. Every one of those activities is described in the life of Christ as well as His disciples. Normalizing the imitation of biblical champions is a valuable lesson for young disciples-to-be. It provides them with an accessible and authoritative source of insight into how disciples behave.

Part of the growth experience is about having a plan for making progress. Do what you can to encourage your emerging disciple to incorporate these activities into their plan.

Accountability for those actions is also useful for converting a random religious practice into a spiritual habit.

LOVING OTHERS

Another level of producing spiritual fruit is achieved by loving other people. For many Americans, this might be the toughest factor of all.

What does this entail? If we return to Paul's description of the fruit of the Spirit and think about these attributes in relation to other people, some possibilities come to mind.

- Because love is not primarily an emotion but an act of caring, serving the needs of others is a tangible demonstration of *love*.

- Every time you encounter a person who is going through difficult times, or experiencing some type of distress, supporting them in word and deed is an act of *kindness*.

- To produce *peace* with fellow followers, accept differences of opinion or lifestyle (as long as those differences are in harmony with scriptural principles), and go to whatever lengths are necessary to resolve any conflicts.

- God blesses His followers frequently. One of the best ways to build community among disciples is to rejoice in the victories or the gains disciples enjoy. Let their *joy* be your joy.

- Everyone processes information differently and at a different pace. If a fellow disciple is slow to grow, displaying *patience* toward that person is an expression of love.

- One of the benefits of being in a community of disciples is the opportunity to share spiritual insights or wisdom with other members. That is part of being *faithful* to the body: sharing new knowledge and wisdom with the people who belong to the family of disciples.

- A natural human tendency is to gossip or to criticize people who make mistakes or do things differently than you would. One of the fruits a disciple manifests is *self-control* in such situations—reining in his tongue or cutting others some slack.

If you work at it, you could make a long list of ways in which you could show God at work in you, bearing the fruit of the Spirit, and controlling your head, heart, and spirit. Those are the types of behaviors to identify with your young disciple, and to jointly put into practice.

MAKING BEHAVIORAL PROGRESS

How do we know whether a child under our tutelage has made sufficient progress on the journey to be deemed a disciple? One of the filters to use in that determination comes from the way Jesus warned a group of enthusiasts in Jerusalem to measure themselves: "If you do not carry your own cross and follow me, you cannot be my disciple."[69] He was telling them, using a cultural reference they understood, that if they did not submit to Him and His ways, they were not qualified to be a disciple.

As we work with children toward making them disciples, we will do well to regularly be asking ourselves if we are leading them to a place of total submission to the will and ways of the Lord. Anything short of that renders us unqualified to accept the title "disciple."

In fact, the issue of knowing where our disciples-in-training stand in the quest to be an acceptable follower of Jesus leads us into our discussion in the next chapter about accountability.

DISCIPLE-MAKING PRACTICE #4
MEASURE, REINFORCE, REPLICATE, AND REJOICE

My studies over the years have indicated that few Christians have a viable accountability system in place. These days the accountability process that most adult believers allude to is their participation in a church-based small group. However, most small groups are more likely to ask if anyone needs prayer for a felt need than to work with its members to evaluate their spiritual experience and how well they are upholding the ways of the Lord.

That's a mistake a disciple-maker ought not to make when mentoring a young person. The more a child embeds personal accountability for their spiritual beliefs and practices into their lifestyle, the more likely they are to be a legitimate representative of the kingdom of God on Earth—and the better prepared they will be to handle God's examination of their life.

It always surprises me when I receive pushback on this from believers. "Why should I answer to her? She's just another human being like me. She has no right to meddle in my affairs." "It's really nobody else's business what's going on in my life. That's between me and the Lord." "I don't owe anyone an explanation for anything I do. I'll answer for my choices on Judgment Day." "He's no better than I am. We're all sinners. I have no duty to share my secrets with him, or any other Christian." "The moment I share what's going on in my life it'll just be fodder for gossip."

That's just a sampling of some of the responses I've heard. And every one of them is understandable but little more than a rationalization.

First, any person who is serious about becoming more like Jesus needs to keep the guidelines and the quality of their life performance in mind. A phrase I commonly use when working with ministries is, "You get what you measure." In other words, if it's important, track how well you are accomplishing that outcome; if it doesn't matter, then don't bother.

Get the facts and decide how well you're doing; don't just roll through life like a pinball reacting to the resistance of the environment around you. Be strategic and intentional in everything you do. Measurement aids you in that process.

Becoming more like Jesus is of supreme importance. If a child is trying to become a disciple of Christ, then she must understand that the only way to grow is not by relying on her feelings about her progress but upon more reliable and objective assessments. She will eventually answer to God for everything she does. Getting feedback before that evaluation will be invaluable in guiding her to better choices and more consistent resistance to temptations and evil.[70]

Remember, the goal with a young person is to form their spiritual life through the development of good habits. Responding to reliable feedback from those who know better and love you is of tremendous value.

Second, it is the job of a spiritual coach to evaluate how well her protégé is doing. How can you help a person grow if you don't know how they're doing? That's the blind leading the blind. And how can you expect them to change for the better if you don't provide wise guidance?

The Bible notes that a follower being equipped for good service has a responsibility to get the facts about their spiritual performance and to change accordingly. Consider this passage:

> Obey your spiritual leaders and do what they say. Their work is to watch over your souls, and they are accountable to God. Give them reason to do this with joy and not with sorrow. That would certainly not be for your benefit.[71]

So yes, the protégé has an obligation to seek out honest feedback and to accept any critiques with a good attitude and a determination to improve. The passage suggests that the disciple-in-training should want to make the discipler proud, which will encourage them to continue to invest in the less-mature follower.

But this passage should send chills down the spine of any of us who are striving to disciple a nascent Christ follower. Note that the Lord warns us we are not simply trying to help someone do what's right and do it better for the sake of being a better person. Our effort has eternal consequences; it impacts their soul. And not only are *they* accountable to God for what *they* do, but *you* are accountable to Him for how well *you* shape the life of that disciple. What an awesome opportunity—and mind-blowing responsibility.

BEING A GOOD MENTOR

Let's remember the context in which any kind of spiritual accountability happens. Your commitment to the young disciple-to-be is to coach them in their faith. You are not seeking to simply facilitate someone who likes going to church, reading the Bible, and attending small groups. While that's the widely accepted view of a "devoted Christian" in America, the research indisputably shows that such a profile leaves people far short of the depth of spirituality that characterizes true disciples.

In the expression of Pastor Kyle Idleman, we are not supposed to merely be "fans of Jesus." We are supposed to be full-fledged imitators of Christ.[72]

As the spiritual coach to a young person, hoping to prepare that child to become a lifelong spiritual champion for the kingdom of God, your job is to lead the child beyond the popular and superficial to the uncommon, deeper life in Christ.

Do whatever it takes to prevent the child from being sidetracked by pop Christianity. Do whatever you can to support them taking the deep dive into the life of a genuine disciple of Jesus—living like Jesus because they fervently believe like Jesus.

Toward that end, be concerned about what they believe because those beliefs determine what they do, and it is through what they do that they become visible and influential Christians. As a discipler, you make a substantial investment into that person's life through a dynamic relationship. You model the disciple's life for them to watch and consider. You observe the protégé's life. You discuss scriptural principles together. You listen to her concerns, questions, and processing of her growth experience. You love her, but you give her space to experiment and own her growth process. You enjoy being with her, largely because you are proud of her continuing commitment and progress. You track how she is doing in relation to developmental goals. You always remember that her efforts are undertaken in the context of spiritual war, so you are quick to praise and slow to criticize. You are honest but sensitive in sharing your feedback, never wanting to break her spirit but always seeking to serve His Spirit in the quest for spiritual maturity.

As that type of mentor, you realize you cannot grow if the two of you do not agree upon specific standards and constantly examine her performance in light of those standards. It can be done, and can only be successfully done, in a way that makes the developmental process enjoyable, rather than a relationship based on fear and rigidity.

MAKING MEASUREMENT WORK

The young disciple must be taught the importance of consistent self-evaluation. To do so requires standards against which to measure performance. That implies goals, which is something the disciple-maker can help the younger follower develop.

The discipler can also help with the measurement process itself, offering a regular series of insights into how the disciple-to-be is doing. As the mature and immature disciples undertake the evaluation together, the objective is to reinforce what's working and redirect that which is not.

As a mentor, your job is not to pass judgment; only God can be justified in judging people. Your responsibility is to pass along life-giving guidance and encouragement that leads to growth.

But how can you reliably facilitate and convey an evaluation that is both upbeat and honest? Here are four common tactics for effective evaluation.

OBSERVATION

The most obvious approach is for the mentor to watch the protégé and simply discuss what she sees happening. Is this subjective? Yes. Does that discredit the advice? Not at all.

Our spiritual performance is always subjective. When it comes to measuring how well we are doing, the most subjective evaluation of all is our self-assessment—our personal sense of progress or regression. Our self-assessment both benefits from, and is diminished by, the countless bits of information we consider that nobody else even knows about.

The best thing about our self-assessments is that they indicate we are self-aware and have chosen to take growth seriously. The worst part about our self-evaluations is that they are often the least reliable review of our performance that we have available.

When we receive input from someone else, their views tend to be considerably more objective and unbiased. They may not understand the many nuances involved in our situation, but their diagnosis is invaluable. We don't have to embrace it in full, but we should earnestly consider that input.

As an evaluator of a disciple-in-training, we may wish to offer our feedback along with a caveat or two. The ultimate analysis is up to the individual. Offering a perspective on what we observe is simply one significant data point for their consideration.

What does a mentor look for? How well does the young person's behavior reflect biblical principles and commands, starting with the seven cornerstones and building toward a more complete biblical worldview?

During the early, highly formative years, your feedback may be most impactful when it relates directly to the core principles of a disciple. A good mentor is searching for evidence of wisdom and growth, not perfection.

We are all human and sinful; the best we can hope for is excellence, not perfection. Crushing the spirit of the young believer serves no purpose. You add value when you encourage growth by engaging them in conversations about what you observed and distilling what was in the mind and heart of the protégé, enabling them to refine their efforts to mimic Jesus.

CONVERSATION

The mentor has many opportunities to discuss the actions of their younger colleague. There are times to discuss questions the younger person raises; times to interact over a Scripture passage or principle the two of you have been studying; times to reflect on how other people handle situations, how the young learner might have responded in that situation, and what can be gleaned from how the other person handled the situation; or times to address an observed behavior of the youngster.

Never forget that the key to discipleship is maintaining a trust-based relationship. Abusive dialogue or heart-wrenching criticism is unfruitful. You are a disciple when you love other disciples, even those just starting down the pathway to holiness. Always demonstrate your love for the mentee and treat them the way you want to be treated by your mentors. Yet discipleship is about tough love—always sharing with gentleness but honesty, forthrightness but humility. Remember that her success is your success.

GOD'S INPUT

Sometimes we forget that this is not about the protégé or you. It's all about God and how well we can honor Him through our lives. That being true, we can be assured that He will provide feedback as well through His Holy Spirit.

One of the great challenges, then, is for both parties to be sensitive to input from the Spirit. As God's advocate, we know that the Spirit will always be present and, therefore, can nudge us in ways that nothing else is able to.

Introducing young followers to the still, small voice of the Lord is one of the more difficult tasks for a mentor. While there is a lack of consensus about the issue, it may well be that many young children are not capable of grasping the existence of a constant spiritual presence who cannot be seen or heard yet communicates with us. Educators contend that children are not able to grasp abstract ideas such as a "Holy Spirit" until later in their adolescent years.

Nevertheless, preparing young disciples to receive God's guidance in ways that the world neither recognizes nor affirms is a valuable lesson about the nature of God and His presence in our lives.

Indeed, expecting and recognizing God's presence in our life is a major distinction between a disciple and a citizen of the world. The more effectively you enable a young disciple to grasp such distinctions—and to share such moments from your own experience with them—the more normal and desirable the omnipresence of God will seem to them.

MEASUREMENT TOOLS

There are a variety of spiritual growth tools that can help believers become more Christlike. None of them are infallible, but many of them have benefited from sufficient testing that they are valuable mechanisms for facilitating spiritual development and have a sufficient history of positive user reviews to commend their use.

Among the kinds of tools that are available are:

- **Worldview Assessments.** Every human being has, and needs, a worldview; the question is which worldview does the individual possess. Worldview examinations typically are designed to indicate whether you have a set of beliefs that are purely and robustly biblical. Each of the worldview surveys I've seen offered online measures worldview differently, although all but one that I have seen focus solely on beliefs, to the exclusion of treating behavior as the proof of worldview.[73]

- **Spiritual Gifts.** Every person is given supernatural abilities by the Lord to facilitate their service to the kingdom of God. These evaluations seek to identify which gifts the Lord has provided to an individual, which will then help guide them toward a life in which they can use those special abilities to serve Him more effectively.

- **Personal Strengths.** The objective of these tests is to identify what types of tasks a person has been created to master. These strengths are often a combination of spiritual gifts and natural abilities. A significant value of identifying one's personal strengths is to gravitate toward opportunities that enable one to provide the greatest value to others and enjoy the experience the most.

- **Personality Attributes.** The insights from these assessments can help someone to better understand themselves and to apply their attributes to life situations and relationships more effectively. The results might also point to areas of personality that the individual may wish to reshape to be more honoring to God.

- **Spiritual Growth and Maturity.** These inventories run the gamut, evaluating factors such as spiritual knowledge, religious behaviors, adherence to the Ten Commandments, service to others, and other measures. These particular models are more subjective and selective in their assessments but may provide useful insights.

DISCIPLES MAKING DISCIPLES

One of the ways that a disciple-in-training can become more adept at following Christ is by enlisting peers to become disciples and helping to disciple those friends. Although some adults get exasperated at such a suggestion—"How can a kid lead another kid on a journey they have not mastered?"—my research has consistently found that many of the most effective evangelizers in America are adolescents. We discovered that they get excited about what Jesus has done in their own life and want to share the good news with friends and family.

Based on the relationship their peers have with the emergent followers of Jesus, and having witnessed changes in his life, his buddies are often caught up in the joy and sign up for the ride.

Granted, a child who is being discipled may struggle with the responsibility and substance of discipling a friend, but at the very least, they can engage their peers in the commitment and help them to find a more mature follower who will pick up the discipling process.

A young child sharing his understanding of the journey and attracting his friends to get involved is no different than teachers who admit that the best way for them to learn a subject is to teach it. When a new follower engages a potential follower in a conversation about the faith journey, the disciple-in-training may gain a more profound understanding of their own transformation due to having to articulate their unfolding spiritual experience. It is common for teachers and mentors to note gaining new insights or clarity simply by having to address the comments and questions encountered while mentoring someone else.

One way to facilitate disciples making disciples is to encourage your trainee to talk to their friends about what they are learning and experiencing in the discipleship process, and to explain the difference it is making in their life. That's one way of upholding Paul's declaration that he was "not ashamed of the gospel" despite the cultural resistance to Christian principles and the persecution his fervor for Christ brought on.

Neither the discipler nor the child being discipled needs to be obnoxious about their spiritual growth in interactions with friends and family. Sharing naturally, from their enthusiasm about their experience, is a great approach.

Remember that stories are a crucial resource in discipling a young person, so your willingness to divulge your personal stories about reaching out to other people—stories with positive endings as well as those with unfortunate outcomes and the lessons you learned from those episodes—will likely be more motivating to the young person than simply applying pressure to share their testimony because "it's the right thing to do and part of your growth process."

ENJOY THE RIDE

Becoming a disciple of Jesus in America these days is no simple task. Standing strong for biblical principles and portraying a lifestyle is no longer the norm; some neighbors and associates will view such behavior in a negative light. But we do not follow the paths prescribed by God to please the world; we do it to please God.

When your disciple-in-training says or does something that shows progress, celebrate the moment. Positive reinforcement is a great way to cement a thought or action in the mind and heart of the child. It also shows that you are paying attention. And it conveys the notion that the Christian life is a joyous life, not a downcast life of limitations and punishments.

God takes pleasure in our acts of obedience, and we should look for opportunities to rejoice when our fellow believers do things according to the book. Actions that correspond to scriptural directives deserve to be cheered on.

SECTION THREE

FAMILIES AND CHURCHES IN PARTNERSHIP

From a biblical vantage point, there are two entities that share the responsibility for preparing young people to be disciples of Jesus: parents and their communities of faith.

The Bible assigns the primary responsibility to parents; they are called to be the chief disciplers of their children. The Scriptures indicate that raising a spiritual champion takes more than the provision of spiritual information and experiences. It includes leadership from the parents in a variety of other life dimensions that also influence the spiritual outcomes of those children.

To help parents in that development process, a local church has the privilege of preparing parents to make disciples of their children. In that sense, the local body of believers is not supposed to be a spiritual holding tank or babysitting service while the parents do adult-oriented faith activities with the other adult believers. The church to which parents belong has an obligation to support parents as they disciple their children. That kind of support happens in various ways.

Working together, parents and their faith community can be a dynamic and potent force for the kingdom of God, leading to transformed lives among the young people in the church's families. In this section, we will examine what is being done, what could be done, and how well those things are being done by both parents and churches.

08

PARENTS MUST MANAGE MEDIA EXPOSURE

As mentioned earlier, exposure to media is the most significant shaper of a person's worldview. This is attributable to a variety of converging factors: the assumed authority of the content developers and presenter, the impact of the presentation format, the peer popularity of the content or platform, the repetition of the message, the seamless blending of entertainment and education, and the receiver's assumption of the veracity of the content provided.

Given the overwhelming persuasive capacity and influence of media vehicles that target children, it is important that parents consciously fill the role of media gatekeeper. The failure to do so gives the media world unrestricted entrée to the mind, heart, and soul of their child.

Secular media creators and marketers are not necessarily bad people developing media with evil intent. However, it is equally true that most media creators do not love your child, care about the spiritual implications of the content they create, share the same spiritual beliefs and moral sensitivities that you possess, or receive awards and reputation based on how well they advance the kingdom of God.

Most content creators are not considering your child's welfare when producing content. Rather, they are developing stories and presenting a particular worldview based on their beliefs or interests while promoting their own goals around money, fame, ideology, morality, political agenda, and so on.

The typical adolescent in America will spend as much time devoted to media consumption each day as they will schoolwork or sleep.

The typical teenager will spend most of their waking hours absorbing messages and visual cues from a variety of media.[74] Allowing that to happen is tantamount to handing your child over to the enemy of her soul and asking them to twist her mind and heart. No Christian parent thinks that is what they are doing, nor would they want to, yet by our relative indifference to how our children spend their time, and our general ignorance about the media they consume, that is essentially what we are doing.

Neuroscience research tells us that large doses of media consumption change the configuration and capacity of the brain[75]—for the worse. Mental health research informs us that anxiety, depression, and anger typically increase with larger amounts of exposure to certain types of media content.[76]

Family research has indicated that when a child spends too much time with popular media, acceptance of parental authority drops.[77] Even the research regarding the sad state of physical health among children has identified excessive media attentiveness to rates of obesity.[78] In fact, there has yet to be any credible research that reveals heavy media consumption by young children, adolescents, or teenagers is beneficial to their life.

If you are going to effectively parent your children, doing whatever it takes to raise them to become spiritual champions, then you must manage their media choices and time commitment. Let's begin by examining why this matters so much by reviewing the content in the most popular media vehicles to which millions of children are exposed every day.

POPULAR TELEVISION CONTENT FOR CHILDREN

The Cultural Research Center performed a content analysis on some of the most popular television programs viewed by children. The programs we studied included the following:

- *Gravity Falls*, available via Disney+, Hulu, Prime Video, and Apple TV, is popular among children two to eleven years old.

- *Miraculous: Tales of Ladybug and Cat Noir*, available on the Disney Channel, is popular among children seven to eleven years old.

- *Magic Mixies*, offered on YouTube TV, is popular among children six to ten years old.

- *Moon Girl and Devil Dinosaur*, seen on Amazon Prime, Disney+, and Apple TV, is geared to children eight to twelve years old.

- *The Secrets of Sulphur Springs*, seen on the Disney Channel, targets viewers six to eleven years old.

- *Doogie Kamealoha, M.D.*, also offered on the Disney Channel, is aimed at children ten to seventeen.

- *The Owlhouse*, another Disney Channel program, is designed for children seven to twelve.

These seven programs, chosen for analysis based on their popularity and availability, are just a drop in the bucket of the hundreds of child-targeted television shows accessible to young people and their families. As you will see, though, media influences such as these shows invariably sidestep the biblical worldview in favor of other philosophical approaches to life.

Although they are designed as entertainment vehicles to keep children engaged with the network, and thus retain subscriber and advertiser revenues, every media vehicle is built upon worldview assumptions. This is because programs feature decisions by their characters, and every decision is based on a worldview, generally that of the writers, directors, producers, and other creative talents behind the scenes who make these shows what they are.

One of the peculiar realities of television programs is that each episode tends to be watched by a child viewer multiple times. The effect is that the underlying worldview is therefore pounded into the mind and heart of the young viewer due to familiarity and repetition.

Children, who still wrestle with the difference between reality and fantasy, and who rarely question the content their parents allow them to view, are the innocent victims of horrific worldview teaching communicated through the themes and actions portrayed through vivid color, fast action, and clever dialogue in all the programs to which they are exposed.

A parent who fails to screen television, movie, social media, musical, or video game content to which their children will be exposed, becomes an unwitting accomplice in this onslaught on the sensitivities of their child.

GRAVITY FALLS

While this show is most heavily influenced by Eastern Mysticism, it also flashes traces of Secular Humanist, Nihilistic, and Postmodern thinking on occasion. There is little-to-no evidence of the biblical worldview in these storylines. In fact, this program typically replaces most biblical themes with a variety of alternatives.

The show emphasizes elements such as magic and demons as it promotes science and human reason rather than God and biblical truth. It does not shy away from the concept of spiritual power, but it never alludes to the presence of a holy, omnipotent, and omniscient Creator God. The stories sometimes suggest evolution and question whether life is reality or illusion. The program does promote loyalty to family but also promotes moral relativism and the absence of a knowable future after we die on Earth.

MIRACULOUS

This show is the greatest example of syncretism in substance, switching between multiple worldviews throughout each episode. While Biblical Theism gets the short end of the stick (the show does discuss the value of forgiveness, although no scriptural reasons are given in support of that recommendation), elements of Postmodernism, Secular Humanism, Eastern Mysticism, and Moralistic Therapeutic Deism are regularly promoted to the young audience.

There are all kinds of lessons taught that conflict with biblical teaching, including sexual confusion, moral relativism, the goodness of humanity, and sources of power and authority other than God (such as crystals). Family is portrayed positively, but it is not a reliable source of developmental guidance for young people in this series.

MAGIC MIXIES

This program is typically written within the framework of the Postmodern and Eastern Mysticism worldviews. Like many children's shows, especially those related to Disney, magic is a big element of the storyline, claiming that the problems of the teen girl who is the main character (Sienna) can be magically whisked away with the help of crystals, her crystal ball, and a magic wand, casting spells that address personal needs.

The most important book in this series is not the Bible; it is the book of magic spells. This fits the notion that there is a universal force at play, but no episode comes close to suggesting that the God of Israel is the greatest and sole loving supernatural power in the universe.

There are positive lessons taught in various episodes about family, teamwork, and friendships, but the fundamental theme is that life is about controlling and enjoying life with family, friends, and supernatural powers.

To make the mystical powers even more alluring, this series has launched a massively successful line of toys, including the Magical Mixies Magical Mixing Cauldron, for crafting spells, and the Magical Mixies Magical Misting Crystal Ball. These toys have been a major crossover sensation on social media as well. Videos that show children and adults using the toys gain in excess of 600 million views on TikTok, replete with claims that the toys can help their users to "experience real magic."

MOON GIRL AND DEVIL DINOSAUR

This series first aired post-pandemic and appears to be another Disney attempt to subtly teach a progressive point of view. The programs shift between Secular Humanist and Eastern Mystical ideals. Science and human reason are highly esteemed as the heroine relies on technology and the scientific method to lead her to the answers to life's complexities. Interpersonal truth and morality are portrayed as outgrowths of cultural relativism.

Not surprisingly, given the context, personal identity is not a gift determined by God but a matter of personal choice. Social justice, tolerance, racial equality, and other popular progressive views are upheld in these storylines.

To their credit, the creators of the show recognize the existence of evil, but they overcome it through human-derived solutions. An early tip-off to the dangers of this series is offered in the theme music, which spouts lines of humanist philosophy: "Everything you need is inside you," along with allusions to our "superpowers" within us.

THE SECRETS OF SULPHUR SPRINGS

The hero of this program is a ghost hunter. The primary worldview is Eastern Mysticism, so a viewer will witness incense, crystals, spirit guides, time travel, discussions of séances, and more in this adventure.

Like an increasing number of child-oriented television shows these days, lying is a regular feature of the characters, with no hint that verbal deceit is unacceptable behavior.

Family is a positive feature of the program, but the depiction of family is of a group of people who justifiably manipulate each other to get what they want.

DOOGIE KAMEALOHA, M.D.

As the name suggests, this program is a takeoff on the 1980s TV hit series, *Doogie Howser, M.D.* The young lady who is the center of the plot models hard work as she balances being a doctor, attending school, and maintaining good relationships with her family and friends.

Unfortunately, the dominant worldview in her story is Postmodernism. The show teaches that each of us must be responsible for determining our own truth. Thus, truth is situational, and morality is conditional. Knowledge is based on social constructs and experiences. The heroine, who is a doctor, teaches that nobody can know what, if anything, happens to us after we die.

The best way to live, according to this show, is determined by the individual, not God. Only we know what is best for us, and we must make our choices wisely. Doogie seeks to achieve fairness, social justice, tolerance, and other outcomes based on her decisions and her personal pursuit of goodness.

Not surprisingly, as a doctor, she also upholds the unassailable value of science and technology. Human reason, based on the scientific method and its resulting facts, trumps any other source of truth. Without any belief in moral absolutes, the questionable language used occasionally (and in the background music) is a natural fit. The character's ongoing interest in sex is another hindrance for a program geared to adolescents.

THE OWLHOUSE

This animated series relies heavily on Eastern Mysticism, featuring magic, witchcraft, demonic creatures, and other dark powers. But the show does not limit itself to New Age-type principles as it delves into several other worldviews as its storylines unfold. Postmodernism, Nihilism, and Secular Humanism are also given airtime.

Overall, the life philosophy spun by this tale is syncretism at its best—multiple worldviews competing for supremacy, regularly conflicting with each other, and ultimately providing little beyond confusion and a sense that anything goes. Biblical morality is rejected in favor of a feelings-based, ends-justifies-the-means approach to right and wrong.

There is talk about predestination, varying ideas about life after death, support for environmentalism, hyper-individualism, the devaluation of human life, and more. Perhaps knowing that the goal of the main character is to become a witch is all you need to know about what kind of worldview training this series will offer to children.

Again, these seven television series geared to children and adolescents are not necessarily representative of all the television series designed for that age group. However, as a small sampling of the shows that are most popular with the target demographic, they highlight some of the dangers of which parents and guardians must be aware.

VIDEO GAMES ARE A BIG DEAL

Years ago, video games were innocuous. When games like PacMan and Donkey Kong ruled the emerging industry, there were no passionate arguments raging about the potential harm such games could do to users. Those days are long gone. The video games industry today far eclipses the hallowed movie industry in gross revenues,[79] and roughly one out of every three people on the planet plays video games during the course of a year.[80]

PacMan and his ilk gave way to more sophisticated games played on computers, eventually incorporating people in different locations playing against each other thanks to internet access. But even that era has largely come to an end. These days, most video games are played on mobile phones or tablets.

Your child is likely one of them. The COVID pandemic of 2020–2022 changed a lot about how we live, and one of those significant changes was the role of video games in society. Due to the lockdowns and severely diminished personal interaction that children had with each other, video games emerged as a digital playground for millions of children. Those games provided them a way to interact with peers, often producing lasting relationships that blossomed post-pandemic.

In fact, 60% of parents claimed that video games were a useful tool for them and their children to remain connected with friends and extended family.[81] During the COVID era, video game playing between parents and their children grew by nearly 50%, with three out of four parents saying that being homebound caused them to play video games with their children at least once a week.

Although the research conducted over the past decade does not support the concern that video games produce violent behavior, those games do leave a lasting impression in the heads and hearts of users. That is why the American Psychological Association and the American Academy of Pediatrics continue to recommend that children not be allowed to play violent video games.[82]

Most medical and professional associations tend not to be concerned about the effects of exposure to sexual behavior, coarse language, corrupt morals, or depictions of potentially addictive behaviors on children, but you should. If they are concerned about violence because it makes an impression, you can be confident that exposure to graphic demonstrations of those other unacceptable behaviors leaves just as significant an impression, whether the gatekeepers worry about it or not.

To be fair, I realize there are benefits that can be realized through video games. They are often used for educational and training purposes, especially in the military and medical fields. Increasing numbers of schools are incorporating video games into their daily classroom and homework activities. There is no doubt that video games can also be used to advance biblical principles and teach scriptural content effectively.

Recent research has confirmed that video games can expand brain matter, improve memory formation, develop strategic thinking, increase fine-motor skills, improve pattern recognition, build system thinking capacity, increase patience, upgrade situation awareness, facilitate better problem-solving, advance literacy, and develop socialization skills.[83] In other words, video games can be a tool for good, if they're used that way and are properly managed.

But as is the case with television programs and movies, parents must be savvy about the media their children use. My examination of this field suggests that simply relying upon industry ratings is an insufficient safeguard to watching out for your children.

Realize that playing video games does alter their brain. That's not necessarily bad; it could be delivering some of the benefits listed above. But applying lax supervision of what your child plays, whom they play with, and how much time they play video games is asking for trouble—and evidence of inadequately protecting your child in the effort to raise a spiritual champion.

If you allow your child to play video games, check each game out thoroughly before giving them your permission. One resource that can help is the website of the Entertainment Software Ratings Board (esrb.com). But here's the caveat: They are the video game industry's professional organization, so they go easier on their standards than you and I might.

However, once you understand their rating system, which is explained on the website, you have your first clue about games that are viable and not viable for your child. Even more helpful, though, are the articles in their blog section. Those articles provide more comprehensive reviews of dozens of popular video games.

But don't stop there. Next, take advantage of websites that provide a Christian perspective on games. Find one or two sites you feel you can trust and turn to them when you are considering giving your child permission to use a new game. Examples of sites to consider would be ChristCenteredGamer.com, ChristianAnswers.net, and GodMindedGaming.com.

AN APPROACH TO MEDIA MANAGEMENT

Every additional form of media you consider—social media, pop music, movies, books, art, magazines, and even newscasts—is a potential minefield for children. Granted, there is helpful content in each of those platforms or genres, material that will help your child to grow stronger, smarter, deeper, more aware, and most importantly, more like Jesus. But every medium also contains imagery and dialogue that will negatively affect the child's self-view and worldview.

You cannot protect them from everything, but you can protect them from most things. That means one of your parenting duties is to act like a military scout, scouring the environment for potentially harmful experiences and doing whatever you can to either shield them from encountering those elements or preparing them to successfully handle them. That kind of scouting and preparation does not effectively occur without a plan.

For several years, ever since identifying media as the top influence on the worldview of children—more than parents, teachers, churches, peers, and siblings *combined*—we have been exploring the most effective ways for parents to manage the media use of children. The result is a simple concept that is challenging to implement but effective. In a nutshell, here is the guideline, known as the four M's of Media Management:

1. *Monitor* media use.

2. *Minimize* media use.

3. *Moralize* media content.

4. *Model* media standards.

Let's break this down, one practice at a time. The central mindset you must own in this process is simple: You are the parent, so you are in charge. Your child will challenge your authority, tweak your emotions, question your faith, and test your stamina. So remember the context: You are at war, not with your child (although it will sometimes seem like it), but against Satan and his destructive plans for you and your child. Be armed and alert, and do not question your role as the responsible one. Once your child arrived on planet Earth, the luxury of questioning your role evaporated.

So begin with the simplest of the four M's: *Monitor* how much media and which media your child will experience. There are no universal assumptions you must accept regarding their media use. Therefore, you may dictate *if* the child can use *any* media, which media, when, and for how long. Naturally, the boundaries you establish are only effective if you consistently monitor the process to be sure your rules are being followed without deviation.

Too much media intake is bad for anyone, so the second M is to *minimize* their media exposure. Think of all the productive ways your child could use her time; media consumption is just one of many options for her day. Place a time limit on how much media she ingests each day, and do not feel bad if the boundary you set seems restrictive by the world's norms. A half-hour a day? An hour a day? The amount of time is up to you, not your child, not their friends, and not society's standards.

Be sure that once you establish the time limit that you stick to your rule. You not only determine how much time, but you must also enforce that boundary, or it becomes meaningless. It's a war. Develop your plan and work it.

The third M, *moralizing* the content to which your child is exposed, may be the toughest factor of all because it means you must analyze the content of the media they will consume. It is your job to provide commentary on what they are exposed to so that they understand the meaning and can place it into a moral context. Media exposure can be a powerful way of teaching right and wrong in very practical ways, but it is mentally taxing and time-consuming.

Most parents feel this exercise is overbearing, too much work, unnecessary, and will breed resentment by the child. In reality, because raising a spiritual champion is your top life priority, and your child benefits from your wisdom and insights, why would you *not* mediate their media content? It's a win-win. And the fact that you must filter the content is a way of making sure they in turn do not devote too much time to media because you sure don't want to spend multiple hours previewing their media content to sift out the garbage.

Your goal is to be sure that no good lesson goes unnoticed and unheralded, and no illegitimate philosophy escapes a scathing but reasoned review. These are wonderful opportunities to regularly introduce biblical content as the basis of your decision-making.

When my wife and I watched movies with our young children and provided worldview commentary during and after each film, our children hated it. Before they finished high school, each one of them separately told us that we had eliminated their joy of watching movies through our insistence on analyzing the moral content of each movie. Given our objective as their parents, their distaste for our intrusion in their entertainment was disappointing, but it did not deter us.

Truth be told (a truth we did not share with them), it wasn't much fun for my wife and me either, but it was part of the job. We had the children, so we were obligated to raise them to know, love, and serve God with all their heart and soul, mind, and strength. Period.

When the Lord takes me home, I will have to give an account for every choice I ever made, including everything I did or did not do as a parent. I know I will have lots of explaining to do, but I am not interested in trying to defend why I let my children determine their media habits and choices without ample supervision and explanation.

The media children receive is always teaching them lessons, whether through visual or audio cues, so providing input as to what is morally right and wrong about the message conveyed is important. We cannot leave those lessons to chance; maybe they would understand the message, but what if they don't? Why take the chance? You are coaching them to become champions; that doesn't happen by chance.

Remember the point made earlier that one of the most effective ways of teaching your child is by demonstrating the principle under consideration through your lifestyle. Let them see the truth in action. The more consistently you *model* the media standards you expect them to live up to, the more seriously they will take your standards and the more likely they are to adopt them.

That's it, quick and easy. It's not rocket science. The real challenge is to conceive a viable plan and then consistently implement that plan.

In case you're wondering, applying the four M's will not win you popularity points with your kids. In fact, they will resent and resist your intrusion into their media world. There will be no end to the complaints about how their friend's parents never do such a thing and how embarrassing this is for them. Turn a deaf ear to the complaints. You are the parent; you are in charge.

Parenting is not a popularity contest. Raising spiritual champions does not happen without battles for control and standards. Parents who have succeeded at raising spiritual champions agreed that their success in this endeavor creates frequent conflict with their children.

For the sake of your own sanity and the maintenance of a viable relationship with your children, you must selectively pick your fights. *Because media absorption will have more impact on their worldview than anything else in our culture, media management is a hill to die on. So do your job as a parent committed to raising a spiritual champion.*

BACKBONE REQUIRED

Make no mistake about it; media options are omnipresent in your child's life, and safeguarding them from the negative influence media can introduce is a daunting, relentless challenge. Effectively managing your child's media exposure is one of the most difficult tasks a parent must master these days.

For at least the last three decades, the creative class in New York and Hollywood has been parenting America's children. From a biblical point of view, they have done a terrible job—but they did the job because very few biological parents tried to stop them. America has essentially handed its children to the media moguls for the last two generations, with the third generation now in progress.

The fact that there are *any* young adults with a biblical worldview in America today is a testament to the fact that a relative handful of people stood strong and resisted the momentum of the media culture. If you are a disciple of Jesus, then you are called to be one of those people.

The only way to fix the problem is not to change the channel or pray that our children will make better media choices. The solution is for you to step up and take control of the media that gets exposure in your house. If you fail to do so, three decades-worth of data persuasively argue that you will fail in your hope of raising a spiritual champion. You will be inviting the reigning culture to raise your child for you.

09

WHERE IS THE LOCAL CHURCH?

America is immersed in a crisis of literal biblical proportions. We are unable to make the choices Jesus would make because we cannot think like Him. We don't know or accept the basic principles on which His choices were made.

Equipping people with the ability to know and apply scriptural principles is the job of the local church. Granted, most Americans no longer have any regular presence in a community of faith, but even when they do, the equipping job is not getting done. How can I make such a claim? Just take a look at an abbreviated profile of churchgoing, born-again Christians:

- 30% strongly agree that they are "deeply committed" to practicing their religious faith.

- Only 29% strongly disagree that absolute moral truth does not exist; therefore, determining moral truth is up to each individual.

- Less than half of all born-again adults believe that Jesus Christ lived a sinless life on Earth or that human life is sacred.

- Large minorities of Christians believe that abortion, for any reason other than saving the life of the mother, is morally acceptable; that consensual sexual relations between adults not married to each other is morally acceptable; and that lying to protect your personal interests or reputation is morally acceptable.

- Only half of born-again adults believe that consistent obedience to God constitutes success. And only half reject the belief that a person who is good enough or does enough good things can earn eternal salvation.

- A mere one out of four (26%) strongly disagree that the Bible is ambiguous in its teachings about abortion, enabling anyone to make a strong biblical argument either for or against abortion.

- Less than half of all born-again adults (45%) read or study the Bible during a typical week.[84]

In the end, the born-again community is not all that different from the rest of the world in many of their beliefs and behavior. How can that be?

There are many explanations. One of the most logical arguments is that spending one hour a week on a church campus, listening to a thirty-minute topical lecture cannot negate or reverse the impact of the cultural ethos in which churchgoers are immersed every day.

An even more powerful argument—one that is a foundation of this book—is that a few sermons a year are highly unlikely to change the minds and hearts of adults because their worldview took ownership of their lives before they became teenagers. Good sermons preached to adults may reinforce appropriate beliefs among those who embrace those perspectives, but are typically too little, too late to introduce wholesale transformation in those lives.

So, what about ministry to children in Christian churches? If their worldview is formed young, and their parents are not helping them to develop a biblical worldview—or at least embrace the seven cornerstones of a biblical worldview—then won't participation in the children's ministry at a Christian church get the job done? That's certainly what millions of parents are hoping. But the reality paints a different picture.

The Cultural Research Center at Arizona Christian University conducted a large, nationwide survey among the pastors of Christian churches. One portion examined the worldview of Senior Pastors. The bottom line is that most Senior Pastors do not possess a biblical worldview—just four out of ten (41%) give evidence of being able to think and act like Jesus.

The inescapable conclusion is, of course, that they cannot give what they do not possess. Therefore, most Christian churches are filled with adults who are not receiving teaching that would point them toward thinking biblically. The big picture is actually a bit worse than that, because others who fill the pulpits—associate pastors and teaching pastors—are even less likely to have a biblical worldview, with a biblical worldview incidence of 28% and 13%, respectively.[85]

But that's what's happening with adults. What about the pastors who lead the ministry to children, where the real worldview development is taking place?

The CRC survey revealed that only one out of every eight children's ministers—just 12%—has a biblical worldview! Sure, it's awful that most adults listen to teaching from pastors who are not consistently biblical, but to expose most children in Christian churches to teaching and programming that is led by ministers who are not consistently biblical is simply criminal.

Here is a brief sampling of just some of the unbiblical beliefs held—and most likely taught—by children's pastors:

- 64% believe there is no absolute moral truth.

- 53% accept reincarnation as a real possibility for them.

- 58% say it is possible to achieve complete spiritual maturity during your lifetime.

- 56% do not believe that sexual relations between consenting adults who are not married to each other are morally unacceptable.

- 61% believe that having faith is more important than which faith you have.

- 58% do not believe that success is best described as consistent obedience to God.

- 74% do not believe that any personal wealth they accumulate has been entrusted to them by God to manage for the benefit of His kingdom.

About half of them believe rather mind-boggling things such as these:

- Jesus Christ sinned while He was on Earth.

- The Holy Spirit is not a living entity that affects lives, but just a symbol of God's power, presence, or purity.

- They would prefer socialism to capitalism.

- They personally chant or repeat a mantra during a typical week.

And a sizeable minority of them argues on behalf of these views:

- 41% say that God gets involved in a person's life only when absolutely necessary.

- 42% do not believe that human life is sacred.

- 44% reject the idea that the purpose of life is to know, love, and serve God with all of your heart and soul, mind, and strength.

- 40% base their moral decisions on guides other than the Bible.

- 43% do not believe that people are born into sin and therefore need Jesus Christ to overcome the effects of sin.

By the way, barely half of them (54%) say that when they die, they are certain that they will live eternally with God but only because they have confessed their sins and accepted Christ as their Savior (i.e., they are born-again, though our surveys do not use that term).

Children's ministers are the poster children for syncretism.

If that doesn't scare you, you're either not a biblical Christian, or you don't understand how discipling your child works.

Think about it. Children's pastors ought to be the best Bible teachers the nation has to offer since they are working with the population segment most likely to incorporate that teaching into their worldview. What a privilege to take part in shaping someone's worldview—and yet we do not even monitor the worldview of the people we place in charge of shaping the worldview of our children.

But let's be fair about this. The fact that so few churches employ children's pastors who themselves possess a biblical worldview is not completely the fault of churches or of the seminaries or Bible colleges that train them. If parents are the "customer" of church-based ministry and have the ultimate responsibility for what their children receive from the church, it's at least partially the parents' fault that most Christian churches are not seeking to develop a biblical worldview among the children.

Churches, like most service-based organizations, are responsive to the expressed needs and desires of their user base. Face it, parents do not clamor for real discipleship experiences for their children, and churches have not done much to push back on that blind spot.

In fact, a few years back, we asked parents the basis on which they evaluate a church's ministry to their children. The most common responses were that parents were seeking programs that satisfy four needs: safety, fun, the potential to meet acceptable friends, and exposure to Christian teaching. A deeper dive into what they sought in relation to "Christian teaching" revealed that parents were interested in their kids learning "how to be a good person" along with some basic information from the Bible.

Granted, we cannot expect parents to use language like "biblical worldview" or even "spiritual formation" to describe what they're seeking for their young ones, since parents are neither familiar with that language nor do they personally possess a biblical worldview or receive teaching that drives them toward one. But startlingly few parents mention lessons like truth, biblical authority, the nature and character of God, sin and salvation, biblical standards for morality, discipleship, and understanding purpose and success, which explains why just 12% of churches have children's ministers who are Bible-oriented.

You get what you measure. Parents seem more determined to evaluate satisfaction with the experience than place value in the substance. Churches seem determined to measure repeat customers and parental satisfaction more than spiritual depth and growth.

LOCAL CHURCH IMPORTANCE

Examining averages can be misleading. The fact that a minority of lead pastors do not have a biblical worldview masks the fact that thousands of churches do have pastors who consistently believe and act in harmony with the Scriptures.

The fact that seven out of every eight children's ministers do not have a biblical worldview can cause us to overlook the one out of eight who does. One way of summarizing this is to admit that a lot of Christian churches in America are not, well, very Christian, but if you search carefully, you can find some that are.

That's the challenge to a Christian parent or guardian of young children. Complete your due diligence to identify a church that can help you raise a spiritual champion.

Let's consider, then, what you need to look for to locate such a church.

First, a good church understands how important children are in the kingdom of God and will do everything it can to support parents in their role as the primary developer of the child's worldview and spiritual life. What might such a church offer, besides affirming words about the importance of children and the desire of the church to help parents? Here is what we found the most effective churches provide:

- Teach and otherwise prepare parents to understand and own the role of spiritual mentor to their child.

- Provide or identify additional resources that will help parents master their role.

- Offer the spiritual support and assistance—prayer, encouragement, wisdom—needed for parents to fight the spiritual war that surrounds parents and their children.

- Help to evaluate the spiritual condition, progress, and needs of their child.

- Facilitate relationships with other parents and with resource people to fortify children on the journey.

- Provide practical, spiritual challenges that the parents are growing in their faith.

- Create opportunities for parents and their children to be Christians together through shared experiences and insights.

Second, what should parents or mentors look for in a ministry to children? In general, the church should seek to bless the children in these ways:

- Establish their parents as their children's chief spiritual coaches.

- Build on the spiritual foundation that parents have initiated.

- Consistently provide age-appropriate teaching of foundational biblical truths.

- Facilitate experiences with the Bible as a user-friendly, valuable guide to life.

- Practice and normalize basic spiritual disciplines, such as prayer, Bible reading, confession, service, stewardship, worship, forgiveness, and gratitude.

- Make it possible for your child to meet and befriend other children who will be good influences and share a similar faith journey.

- Provide an appealing and practical introduction to living a Christian life.

- Offer possible mentors for the children to relate to.

When you find a church that checks these items off the list, you're on to something promising. But don't stop there. You need to dig one level deeper.

EFFECTIVE CHILDREN'S MINISTRIES

The Cultural Research Center also completed a study of churches whose children's ministry is serious about child discipleship. To be honest, identifying such churches was not easy, and finding such places was not common. The only way that will change is if parents become more discerning and demanding consumers.

I am not suggesting that the Christian faith is a commodity to be consumed or that the local church should be treated like a consumer good or institution. I am challenging you to take the discipling of your child so seriously that you will not settle for a church that does not consider that task as high a priority as you do.

We beat the bushes and identified some churches across the country that seem to prioritize discipling children. The children's pastors of those churches were gracious enough to complete very long interviews with us so that we could understand what makes them tick, how they conduct their ministry, their relationship with parents, and what success looks like in those ministries.

Beyond the general profile described above, here are additional insights gleaned from churches that put your child first and consider discipling that child in tandem with the parent (and other disciplers) to be the foremost responsibility of the community of faith.

WHAT THE CHURCH BELIEVES

A good place to start is with the statement of beliefs of the church or the children's ministry. Be careful, for some of these are "boilerplate" declarations that do not align what is actually taught or expected by the church. However, you can be pretty sure that if the statement of faith does not conform to biblical teaching and practice, the church is not likely to be a shining example of Christianity in action despite the statement.

One way to dig a bit deeper into this is to determine which, if any, of the historic creeds or teaching documents the church endorses and abides by. Find out where they stand on traditional prayers or declarations such as:

- The Apostles' Creed—one of the earliest statements of faith accepted by Christians around the world. This is a fundamental statement of belief in the God of Israel, with a basic and balanced depiction of Jesus alongside a healthy view of the Holy Spirit. It reminds us of our place in creation and our reliance upon God for His redemption.

- The Nicene Creed—similar to the Apostles' Creed in some respects, this historical profession of faith is a majestic defense of the divinity of Jesus Christ and the Trinity.

- The Athanasian Creed—a statement of faith that emphasizes the unity, distinctness, and equality of the three Persons of the Trinity as well as the unique nature of Jesus Christ, being both God and man, distinct from God yet united in Him.

- The Lausanne Covenant—ratified in 1974 by leaders of denominations and churches from more than 150 nations. This serves as both an affirmation that the gospel is God's good news for the entire world and a resolution to tirelessly proclaim that good news with an understanding of the nature of God, Satan, and man. With a heavy emphasis on evangelism, it also stresses the necessity of full-gospel discipleship as well.

- The Manhattan Declaration—penned in 2009, this widely embraced document among theologians and church leaders speaks to the sanctity of human life, support for traditional (biblical) marriage to the exclusion of all other unions, and the importance of religious liberty and expression.

Any church, or responsible pastor representing a church, who is unfamiliar with these statements, or unwilling to study them to provide you with feedback, or that rejects any of these may not be the place to bring your child.

WHAT THE CHILDREN'S PASTOR BELIEVES

Before you unleash a church leader on your child, be sure you're comfortable with their faith. Very few children's pastors are literally interviewed by the parents of the children whom she will be influencing. Yet, those same parents will grill an academic tutor, or a specialized coach being considered for their child.

That disconnect is untenable. Job one is to raise a spiritual champion; you cannot enlist a coach who will not help your child advance toward the goal. Just knowing that seven out of every eight children's ministers lack a biblical worldview ought to send shivers down your spine and bolster your determination to find the right spiritual mentor for your child.

Many parents blush and confess that they are not spiritually confident enough to ask theological questions of church personnel. Get over it. If nothing else, quiz them about their beliefs regarding the seven cornerstones—basic biblical Christianity, but not widely embraced Christianity.

Ask follow-up questions to be sure you understand what they believe regarding those foundational principles. Don't accept theological jargon or doctrinal mumbo-jumbo. If you cannot understand what they're telling you, your child won't either. Man up on this point. You don't have to be aggressive or offensive, but you deserve to know what the leader endorses theologically. They should be excited that a parent cares and is willing to discuss such matters without an attitude.

CURRICULUM

The effective children's ministries tend to both rely upon published curriculum and develop some of their own for internal use. Ask about the published curriculum they use to help figure out how serious they are about biblical purity and intentional worldview development.

Ask to see or even take home a sample of the curriculum to evaluate whether it is biblical and appropriate for your child. This is the substance of what your child will receive from the church; do not be shy about examining it.

Remember, most of the people who teach in children's ministry classes, service, and other events are volunteers who will rely heavily upon the curriculum chosen and provided by the church. If the content of the curriculum fails to impress you, forget about safety, friendliness, and good times; this is not the place to frequent.

DEFINE SUCCESS

Each church program has specific outcomes that determine whether the ministry is a success or not. Find out what that definition of success is, and you will have an important clue as to the value of that ministry in your adventure to raise a spiritual champion. If you hear talk about how many children show up, or how happy the children are, be cautious. Those are outcomes that are positive, but they have little to do with whether disciples are being made.

Get a sense of how success is measured. If it is based on the feelings of the person in charge, be cautious. There is no error-proof way of ascertaining the spiritual growth of children, but a leader's intuition is not a reliable indicator of transformative impact.

THE PARTNERSHIP

If the children's ministry does not ask you to participate in what it is doing to minister to children on the church campus, be cautious. The most effective ministries indicated that they had a large majority of the parents engaged in their ministry to young ones and that the ratio of adults to children was very small (typically something close to two adults for every child). That puts an enormous burden on the church to get parents and other adults involved—and that, in turn, means that the church's leadership must be fully and constantly supportive of what happens with the children.

If the children's ministry does not expect you to be driving the discipleship process, be cautious. The effective churches have regular and frequent contact with the parents, to build a symbiotic discipleship process. They send emails or tests each week. They send home portions of the curriculum for the parent and child to complete during the week. They make occasional phone calls to stay up to speed. They use any and all means available to effectively and consistently communicate with the parents to keep the discipleship process active and healthy.

AMPLE RESOURCES

The children's ministry should have what it needs to produce what it needs to accomplish. The most effective children's ministries had:

- a paid staff person overseeing the children's ministry (a full-time position in mid-sized or larger churches, a part-time position in small churches);

- sufficient space to separate children by age groups so that they could be discipled more effectively;

- a sufficiently large—and detailed—budget so that the church leaders could provide what was needed and facilitate accountability;

- passionate and full-orbed support from the church's primary leaders, including both the senior pastor and the ruling lay leadership team (such as elders);

- access to resources needed to recruit a large enough cadre of volunteers to enable the ministry to work as desired.

Every children's ministry is different, but every one of them requires adequate resourcing to be effective. A one-room schoolhouse approach does not seem to work well. If children are the most important "clients" of a local church, then the budget and other resources should reflect it.

VOLUNTEERS

Volunteers are people like you—parents who (probably) do not have extensive theological training but who want a great spiritual experience for their kids. But what is that? How would they deliver that? They generally do not know, so training and good supervision are crucial elements of a great children's ministry. How much, and what type of training, do volunteers receive? And how is the "job performance" of volunteers assessed? What happens to volunteers who are not doing a good job?

HIGH-TOUCH MINISTRY

Every effective children's ministry we encountered majored on building lasting relationships between the people working with the children and the youngsters. The Christian faith is as much caught as it is taught, and you are most likely to notice and imitate the qualities of people you know and trust. This is one reason why small adult-to-student ratios and the commitment of volunteers and staff are critical.

BIBLE-DRIVEN

Many churches seem to think children can be adequately discipled by learning about the Bible—but from extra-biblical resources. The effective ministries have a different view: To be a disciple, you must know and be comfortable with the Bible itself, and that only happens through regular experience with the Bible.

Learning about God is very different from relating directly to God. Similarly, knowing and learning about the Bible is vastly different than touching, reading, studying, and trusting the Bible. Every chance you get, have your children interact with the Bible, even if it is an age-appropriate version.

YOU ARE IN CHARGE

It is a big deal to place your child under the spiritual care of someone else, even for just an hour or two a week. The entire burden of choosing which church to trust to assist you and your child with their spiritual development falls on your shoulders. Your child does not know much about the process beyond whether he likes the teacher, the other kids, the environment, the snacks, and the activities, so it's not their choice to make; it is yours. Don't wimp out and settle for a church just because your child seems happy or the program is well-marketed.

The attributes described above are intended to guide you as you search for a helpful church. You may wish to downplay the importance of some of these items, elevate the significance of others, and add a few factors of your own. Great! *Own this process.* You must do whatever it takes to raise a spiritual champion.

Do not be seduced by the size, reputation, resources, or friendliness of a church. You have been given a life-transforming assignment by your child's heavenly Father. You need partners to help you master that assignment. Use this information to help you plan your effort to identify and link with the best possible partners.

A WORD ABOUT CHRISTIAN SCHOOLS

Like churches, there are roughly 10,000 Christian elementary and middle schools across the nation that exist to assist parents in raising spiritual champions. If you have chosen to not homeschool your children—and few Christian parents do (only about 4% of all elementary and middle-school students are homeschooled, and roughly the same proportion attend a Christian school), then consider whether a Christian day school is right for the child you are mentoring or raising. More than two million elementary and middle school students attend Christian schools.[86]

Based on national averages of how children spend their time, three dominant activities earn the lion's share of the hours on their schedule. Children devote the largest share of their day to sleep, followed closely by time at school, and then time devoted to media content. Once they reach high school, the time invested in school and media are in reverse order.

If you are entrusting a child to another group of adults for more than a thousand hours each year, for up to thirteen years running, carefully consider the impact those educators will have on the worldview of your child.

To the best of my knowledge, there is no credible research profiling the worldview of public-school teachers. However, if the pandemic taught us anything, it showed us that public schools are no friend of Christ. The news regularly contained horrific anecdotes, which have since been discovered to represent more widespread practices concerning the moral, spiritual, philosophical, and sociopolitical garbage our children are being taught in public school classrooms. Anti-scriptural philosophies such as Critical Race Theory (a version of Marxism) have been (and, in some instances, still are) openly promoted by various teachers unions, governments, school boards, and public schools across the nation.

Evaluations of the substance taught in school-approved curricula have been shocking to millions of unaware Christian parents. Subjecting your children to a daily barrage of anti-God, anti-Christian, immoral teaching is untenable.

Be forewarned, not every Christian school teaches biblical truth or seeks to grow students to embrace the biblical worldview. Just as you must carefully vet a church regarding the content it promotes to children, you must do the same with the school that your child will attend, whether it is a public, private, parochial, or Christian school.

Labels are subjective and general; dig beneath the surface to discover first-hand what your child will be taught. If it opposes the biblical worldview, you should be opposed to that school.

A Bible-based Christian school can be an enormous help to a parent who is striving to raise a spiritual champion and partnering with parents in seeking to defeat the prevailing culture that dismisses biblical truths and lifestyles.

We find that children who are homeschooled have the greatest probability of developing a biblical worldview (largely because they also have the highest probability of being raised by a devout biblical Christian). Children who attend Christian schools are the next most likely to develop a biblical worldview. It is possible, but unusual, for children who attend parochial, private, or public schools to become spiritual champions.[87]

It is not the job of a Christian school to raise your child to be a spiritual champion, but it is their job to assist you in discipling that child. Rest assured that you will not find a public school dedicated to raising disciples of Jesus Christ.

When your child passes from this planet and must give an account for his life to God, academic achievements will not be on the agenda; spiritual commitment will. Not every Christian school is geared to producing fully committed followers of Christ, but they do exist, and when you find one, that school is a priceless gift to you.

10
FIGHT
FOR
YOUR
CHILDREN

We have covered a lot of territory in this book. The final challenge is for you to recognize that as the person biblically responsible for raising your child to be a spiritual champion—and remembering that every day is part of a lifelong spiritual war for their heart, mind, and soul—you need to approach their discipleship as battle training.

You must model for them the life of a spiritual warrior, and they must see some of the ugly parts of the battle to begin to grasp what it takes to be a genuine disciple of Jesus. He promised persecution and tribulations; some of those dark moments will surely occur as you seek to train a passionate warrior for the kingdom of God. But He also promised to never leave you or abandon you, and He has promised His power and guidance as you devote yourself to serving Him.

Parenting your child(ren) is one of the most noble and profound ways in which you can serve Him.

PARENTING AS A SPIRITUAL WARRIOR

Those of the Eastern Mystic tradition—one of those popular, non-biblical worldviews—take the concept of spiritual warrior very seriously—perhaps more seriously than we Christians do. To them, a spiritual warrior is one who fights against self-ignorance. That battle is waged to facilitate self-awareness and achieve self-actualization. That makes sense, given that Eastern Mysticism is all about personal enlightenment and unity with the universe. It is all about *self-enriching* and ennobling self.

To us Christians, though, a true spiritual warrior is one who seeks *God's* wisdom and strength, so we may experience harmony with Him. The war is not about us or our accomplishments within it; it is about devotion and service *to Him* and to Him alone. And there is no higher calling He gives you than to prepare your child to know, love, and serve Him with all of their being.

Every moment of every day, you are a spiritual warrior, engaged in the spiritual battle between God and Satan. You are either fighting *for* God or fighting *against* God. As a follower of Jesus, your identity is that of a spiritual warrior. You are fighting for the glory of God. Raising a spiritual champion is your offering to the Lord, your gift of love to Him.

So to be a victorious parent, you must be *equipped* for battle—and consciously equip your children, as well.

That raises the next question—what *weapons* will you use in the war? What is the *arsenal* at your disposal that you will both use in the battle and that you will pass along to your children as they engage God's enemy?

This is important because warfare is about *strategy, tactics, and resources. You* and your children are beloved members of God's family, but you are also combatants serving in the army of God. These weapons are resources that will affect your capacity and personal fate on the battlefield.

The apostle Paul was one of the early Special Forces warriors of the Christian church. He is an example of a terrorist who switched sides in the midst of the war. He went from terrorizing followers of Christ to leading them in the daily war against Satan.

Paul is a model spiritual warrior. Based on training and personal experience, he spoke extensively and knowledgeably about your weapons. These are the weapons you must be exposed to and *master*. You would be well advised to become familiar with Ephesians 6:10–18, where he provides a weapons tutorial.

Paul starts by describing what he called the "belt of truth." Paul sought to be an agent of cultural transformation based on spreading truth. One must know the truth to spread it, so expect to undertake an intense and urgent *search for truth*. That will lead you to God, who is the embodiment and source of all truth. And that, in turn, will lead you to His words in the Bible.

Once you establish your *biblical worldview*, every decision you make has the potential to be in harmony with the principles and commands of God. When you know and represent truth, you are capable of taking every thought captive for Christ.[88] You will be transformed by the renewing of your mind.[89]

You cannot hope to be an agent of transformation until you have allowed God to transform you. You've heard it said that "hurt people hurt people." In like manner, let me suggest that transformed people transform people.

But knowing and adopting truth is a necessary but insufficient condition to be an effective spiritual warrior. Paul then tells us we must also put on the "body armor of God's righteousness." He calls you to be a model of doing what's right.

In other words, to be a great warrior for the kingdom, you must be *obedient* to God's principles and commands. A biblical worldview helps you to know what those principles and commands are, and how they fit together like a puzzle to prepare you for usefulness in service to the king. But a worldview is not just about belief; it is biblical beliefs consistently translated into and demonstrated through your lifestyle.

Your righteous behavior is a showcase of how God transforms human lives. Talk is cheap, but tangible proof of your talk is unassailable. It not only pleases God, but it also stirs those around you. Consistent obedience elevates you to a level of battle most Americans never reach. It promotes you to the elite forces of Heaven.

And keep in mind the importance of behavior that is consistent with biblical beliefs as you model the Christian life for your children. Earlier you read how millions of children dismiss their parents as a worldview influence because their beliefs and behaviors are at war with each other. So not only will harmony in what you think and how you act equip you to serve the Lord on the battlefield of our culture, but that harmony is also crucial to effectively parenting your children.

But to be a worthy adversary of Satan, you need more. Paul then describes the "shoes of peace." That sounds odd, but he is describing a resource that will carry you through the war, namely, the peace of God that surpasses all human understanding. Being reconciled, through Christ, to the Commander in Chief alleviates anxiety about your worthiness to serve or His trust in you as a warrior. Wear the good news like a pair of comfortable shoes.

War is not to be trifled with, and not to be underestimated. It is a game played for keeps. It is a deeply challenging experience, even if you are properly prepared. It is a *terrifying* experience if you are *not* properly armed for the battle.

To fight that battle appropriately, you must be sure that you are doing what's right, for the right side, and for the right reasons. That demands deep confidence in God, which comes from a grace-driven relationship with Him. The confidence produced through that relationship will give you the necessary strength and commitment to wage war.

Paul described this to his audience in Rome when he explained that once we irrevocably choose God's side, He gives us the confidence we need to fight for Him. The fight will still be difficult, but the peace of God will sustain us as it provides endurance. That endurance strengthens our character and resolve and propels us forward in His strength. Paul details that in Romans 5.

But Paul does not stop there. He continues to describe our armory, next talking about the "shield of faith." This is about the support we receive from God's Holy Spirit that enables us to deflect the attacks of Satan and his demons.

As spiritual warriors, God does not want us to be unprepared. He promises that we will face trials, temptations, persecution, and hardships. That's what the war is. It is not easy. It is relentless. It is often brutal. But through a profound faith in God's love, purposes, and protection, we can push forward in His strength to accomplish mighty things for the kingdom.

Remember, the war is *not about you*. But you are offered the *privilege* to participate, and you even get to choose your side. In fact, we know how the war will end, so it almost feels like cheating, choosing the winning side before the conclusion of the war. But there will be *immense challenges* en route to victory, so God is preparing you in advance.

Your next piece of battle gear is the "helmet of salvation." Devote yourself to the cause of Christ, and you will be saved—not on Earth but in eternity. This is the ultimate protection against fear, doubt, imperfection, and self-destruction.

The more completely you grasp the realities of the spiritual war raging around you, the more likely you are to realize you are ill-prepared to do what you are being asked to accomplish. It is only through a *transformational relationship with Christ* that you have access to His power, which is the only power that can withstand the attacks of God's enemy and enable you to gain ground for the kingdom of God through your parenting efforts.

With body armor, a shield, shoes, and a helmet in place, you are almost ready to enter the battle zone. But those are all *defensive* weapons. How can you win a war if you have no *offensive* weapons, nothing to push back with?

You can't.

The final element of your equipment is the "sword of the Spirit," a weapon that cuts through the darkness with the light of God's Word. Your sword is the practical tool of truth, the Bible. If you possess a biblical worldview, you can wisely share elements of that truth in any given battle situation where you are placed.

The words of God, being truth, are capable of shattering the constant lies, confusion, and deceptions used by the enemy. In a world that is uncertain and chaotic, and where the enemy fervently seeks to instill anarchy to eliminate God's order, it is God's wisdom that sustains order, meaning, righteousness, justice, purpose—*and hope*.

Incredibly, God trusts you to fight on His behalf, armed with His truth. There can be no greater privilege—but with that privilege comes great responsibility. That responsibility is developing a thorough knowledge of His words and the boldness to share them and apply them in every relevant situation, no matter the cost.

Paul adds one additional component to your war effort: "praying in the Spirit." No soldier on the battlefield will last long if he is cut off from his commander. There must be constant communication. Effective communication is a two-way conversation.

That is how we must pray. Empty your heart and soul to the Lord, but also fiercely listen to and accept His response. This is an act of submission and trust. As James reminds us, "The earnest prayer of a righteous person has great power and produces wonderful results."[90]

DAILY ROUTINE

Given this call to action, and Paul's invaluable description of warrior preparation, will you commit to doing the following each day, to not only bolster your own capacity as a disciple of Jesus, but also as a parent dedicated to raising spiritual champions?

1. Accept the reality that either you are or are not a warrior for God. Those are your only choices. If you choose to serve God (and never forget that He chose you first), then you are designated to be a disciple of Jesus. That is your identity—a

follower of Christ for the glory of God. If you are uncomfortable because being a spiritual warrior was not on your agenda, get over it. The God who created you and loves you is preparing you for this future.

2. Know that your Father in Heaven never sets you up for failure. He always gives you exactly what you need to accomplish your divine assignment, when you truly need it.[91] So move beyond merely accepting the role—own it. Make an irrevocable, all-consuming commitment to Him. Doing this alone will have a profound impact on your children.

3. Develop peace with God—not a standoff but a resolution and relationship. Confess your sins, ask for His forgiveness and the strength to resist future temptations, and follow Him. Remember, among the marks of a true disciple are placing God above all else in your life, submitting to His authority in all things, and surrendering your life to Him. Once you realize you are not in charge, and you trust Him to love and lead you into fruitful service, life will be much different for you as a servant of God—and a parent capable of raising spiritual champions.

4. Study the Bible. Don't simply read it as if it were a good novel; passionately dig into it and embrace its teachings. God provided His words to you so they might have a transformative effect on you. Take the text seriously and allow the Holy Spirit to renew your mind and soul through them.

5. Ask God to reveal truth to you and for you to be sensitive enough to see it. Our culture is pushing you to look inside yourself to feel your own truth. Don't fall for that deception; the only truth that lies within you is that which God has implanted and the Holy Spirit has revealed. Trust and rely upon God to be your sole repository of truth.

6. Invite His Holy Spirit to guide, protect and enlighten you. Pray in the Spirit. *Get tight with the Holy Spirit.* This is God within you, God working through you. The deeper your relationship with the Spirit, the greater the works He can do through you. It is the presence of the Holy Spirit in you that makes you holy—that is, not *perfect* but *set apart* for the things of God. Give the Holy Spirit free reign in your life, and you will reap the benefits.

7. Live a life of obedience to God. It will not be easy; the Christian life is a countercultural life. You will be mocked and persecuted for your commitment to His ways. Neither waver nor fear in the midst of such commitment; the results may not become clear and uplifting until after your time on Earth is done. Play the long game.

8. Be confident and maintain hope. The choices you make today will have eternal consequences. Your children must experience your unshakeable determination and courage based on your relationship with God. It is not a false or empty hope. The love of Christ is your—and your children's—only hope.

Be forewarned: This commitment, and your investment in training for spiritual war, will inevitably generate *constant and stiff resistance*. Count on it. Anticipate it. Be ready. And be confident that God does not give a faithful soldier more than that warrior can handle. Fight in His strength, not yours, and rest assured that nothing can withstand the strength of God.

Finally, *buckle up and enjoy the ride*. There will be times of blissful victory. There will be times of pain and suffering. But ultimate victory is yours, according to God—and, as the embodiment and definer of truth, you can believe Him.

Wars are won because well-trained, single-minded warriors establish and practice good habits. Raising a spiritual champion is not for the faint of heart, but a spiritual warrior has a strong and courageous heart because they fight for the victorious One. Raising a spiritual champion can be an exhausting and difficult process, but it is also an incredible spiritual adventure and a transformative parenting experience.

So enjoy the process. Bask in the amazing blessing of being counted *worthy* to serve and sometimes *suffer* for His name and to share in His glory. Realize that *He will transform the world through you* and your child if you remain ready and committed. No matter what happens on the battlefield today, when the war is over, *you win*!

APPENDIX

ENDNOTES

CHAPTER 1

1   This information is contained in the book *Helping Millennials Thrive: Practical Wisdom for a Generation in Crisis*, by George Barna, et al. (Arizona Christian University Press: Glendale, AZ, 2023).

2   Averages provided from multiple surveys in the Real Clear Politics tracking summary. "Direction of Country, Real Clear Politics, accessed May 25, 2023, https://www.realclearpolitics.com/epolls/other/direction_of_country-902.html.

3   This data is from the national study, *America's Values*, conducted by the Cultural Research Center at Arizona Christian University, commissioned by AmericasOne. Wave one of the research was conducted in June 2022 among a nationally representative sample of 2,282 adults. More data and commentary from that study are accessible at

www.CulturalResearchCenter.com and at AmericasOne.org.

4   Jeffrey Jones, "U.S. Charitable Donations Rebound; Volunteering Still Down," Gallup, January 11, 2022, https://news.gallup.com/poll/388574/charitable-donations-rebound-volunteering-down.aspx.

5   Aaron Smith, Kay Lehman Schlozman, Sidney Verba, and Henry Brady, "The Current State of Civic Engagement in America," Pew Research Center, september 1, 2009, https://www.pewresearch.org/internet/2009/09/01/the-current-state-of-civic-engagement-in-america/.

6   *American Worldview Inventory 2021*, conducted by the Cultural Research Center at Arizona Christian University, N=2,000 adults, January 2021.

7   This and similar data are accessible at https://www.organdonor.gov/learn/organ-donation-statistics.

8   Solitaire Townsend, "88% of Consumers Want You to Help Them Make a Difference," *Forbes*, November 11, 2018, https://www.forbes.com/sites/solitairetownsend/2018/11/21/consumers-want-you-to-help-them-make-a-difference/?sh=241b3e246954.

9   Data from the national study, *America's Values*, research conducted by the Cultural Research Center at Arizona Christian University, commissioned by AmericasOne; data collected June–July 2022. The two waves of data are based on interviews with an aggregate, nationally representative sample of 3,793 adults. Further data and commentary based on this research are

available at www.CulturalResearchCenter.com and at America-sOne.org.

10 Matthew 28:19–20.

11 John 8:31; 13:35; 15:8; Luke 14:26, 33, 34.

12 See Dietrich Bonhoeffer, *The Cost of Discipleship*, 1949 (2nd ed. reprint, New York, NY: Touchstone Books, 1995).

13 Jesus addressed the cost of discipleship in Luke 14:25–33. The necessity of disciples being repentant is noted in Matthew 4:17; Acts 2:38, and Romans 6:1–2. The necessity of obedience is laid out in Luke 6:46 and James 2:14–26. The end result is that we become a "new creation in Christ," described in 2 Corinthians 5:17.

14 Mark 12:29–30

15 Among the Scriptures to consider in this regard are Deuteronomy 6:1–9; Proverbs 2:1–13; 22:6; 23:13; 29:17; 2 Corinthians 12:14; Ephesians 6:4.

16 Genesis 9:7; Deuteronomy 6:3; Psalm 8:2; 34:11; 103:13; Malachi 2:15; Matthew 18:2–6; 19:13–15; 21:15; Mark 10:13–16; Luke 1:25; Philippians 2:15.

17 Genesis 28:3; Exodus 2:1–10; 12:26, 37; Numbers 5:28; Deuteronomy 4:9–10; 6:1–8; 7:13; 8:5; 28:1–4, 11; 31:11–13; 1 Samuel 20:42; 1 Kings 3:1–3, 16–28; Judges 14:16, 19; Ruth 3:5; Proverbs 1:8–9; 3:11–12; 6:20; 8:32; 13:1, 24; 19:18, 26; 20:7; 22:6; 23:13–14; 24:21; 29:15–17; Psalm 34:11; 78:4–6; 127:3; 145:4; Jeremiah 2:30; 3:22; Lamentations 4:2; Ezra 8:21; Matthew 18:6;

21:14–16; Luke 9:37–43; Acts 2:38–39; Ephesians 6:1, 4; Colossians 3:20; 1 Thessalonians 2:12; Hebrews 12:7–8.

CHAPTER 2

18 If you are not a parent but have, or could have, significant influence on the life of one or more children, then please substitute whatever title fits you better when you see my advice directed to parents. Granted, some biblical responsibilities are aimed squarely at parents, but that does not preclude you from having an important role in the raising of a spiritual champion who is not your child. Grandparents, other family members, teachers, ministers, and others can play such a role in the life of a child. The same information and developmental principles that will motivate and guide parents in their parenting efforts are likely to apply to your participation in the child's life.

19 The source of the statistics in this section is a survey of teenagers, ages thirteen to eighteen, conducted by the Cultural Research Center at Arizona Christian University in December 2022 with a national sample of teens regarding the elements of their worldview. These statistics for young people pertain only to the teenagers who were thirteen or fourteen years old at the time of the survey.

20 The adult data referenced here is from the *American Worldview Inventory*, conducted in January 2023 by the Cultural Research Center at Arizona Christian University among a representative sample of 2,000 adults.

21 Ibid.

22 The most comprehensive description of parenting practices that lead to spiritual champions is in *Revolutionary Parenting* (George Barna, Carol Stream, IL: Tyndale House Publishers, 2007). I have conducted regular updates on that study since its publication and have yet to find significant additions or departures from the original findings. This present book is the most comprehensive update of that previous book and of the research that formed the foundation of *Transforming Children into Spiritual Champions* (George Barna, Grand Rapids, MI: Baker Books, 2016).

23 These statistics are based on a nationally representative survey of 1,000 parents of children under the age of eighteen conducted during December 2022 by the Cultural Research Center at Arizona Christian University. The survey included 334 parents who were born-again Christians. They are labeled "born-again" NOT based on self-identification but on the basis of reporting that they believe when they died they will live eternally in Heaven but only because they have confessed their sins and have accepted Jesus Christ as their Savior.

24 The three surveys included two that were specifically among parents and one in which parents were a large subgroup in a national survey of adults. Overall, the three surveys conducted by the Cultural Research Center at Arizona Christian University in 2022 and 2023 found nearly identical outcomes regarding self-identification with the Christian faith (ranging from 67% to 69%) and

statistically similar outcomes regarding the incidence of a biblical worldview (ranging from 2% to 3%).

25 Syncretism is a worldview that is based on a combination of beliefs and behaviors adopted from other, more uniquely defined and well-known worldviews, such as Secular Humanism, Postmodernism, Eastern Mysticism, Marxism, Nihilism, and Moralistic Therapeutic Deism.

26 *Monty Python and the Holy Grail*, directed by Terry Gilliam and Terry Jones (Python [Monty] Pictures Limited, 1975).

27 The data for adults is based on data from the *American Worldview Inventory 2023*. You can read more about this research in the report, "Incidence of Biblical Worldview Shows Significant Change Since the Start of the Pandemic," Cultural Research Center at Arizona Christian University, released February 28, 2023. The survey among teenagers was also conducted by the Cultural Research Center and is referenced in reports released online by CRC. The nationwide, worldview-related studies conducted by CRC are available for free and can be accessed at www.CulturalResearchCenter.com.

CHAPTER 3

28 The American Culture & Faith Institute ran a series of nationwide surveys among Protestant senior pastors each year between 2014 and 2018. In those surveys, we discovered that most churches measure five elements to determine the success of their ministry:

weekly attendance, amount of money raised, number of staff, number of programs offered, and square footage of the building space on their campus(es). If the figures for each of those measures are higher than they had been fifty-two weeks earlier, the church is usually deemed to be a "healthy and growing ministry."

29 This is based on the results from a series of studies among Protestant pastors conducted by the American Culture and Faith Institute in 2016, 2017, and 2018.

30 "Why Children's Ministry is the Growth Engine of the Church with Dale Hudson," Vanderbloemen, 2022, https://www.vanderbloemen.com/blog/why-childrens-ministry-is-the-growth-engine-of-the-church-with-dale-hudson-podcast.

31 Psalm 8:1–2, Matthew 21:15–17.

32 1 Samuel 3:1–4:1.

33 Matthew 18:1–6.

34 Ephesians 6:1–3.

35 These comments about parenting perspectives and practices are based on several surveys conducted among nationally representative samples of parents of children under the age of thirteen, conducted in 2022 by the Cultural Research Center at Arizona Christian University. More of the statistics from those studies will be shared in later chapters of this book.

36 "Gotta Serve Somebody," lyrics and music by Bob Dylan, performed on the album *Slow Train Coming*, 1979, lyrics copyrighted

through Special Rider Music, http://www.bobdylan.com/songs/gotta-serve-somebody/.

37 This is a general statement that relates to the entire population. Please note that with some niches of the young population, churches have significant influence. Those tend to be children from homes in which the parents are both deeply committed to their faith; the entire family is regularly and significantly involved in church life, experiencing more than an hour per week of church exposure; and in which spiritual habits such as daily family prayer and individual Bible reading and relational prayer are practiced.

38 Proverb 22:6.

39 Galatians 6:7.

CHAPTER 4

40 Crescent B. Martin, M.P.H., M.A., Kirsten A. Herrick, Ph.D., M.Sc., Neda Sarafrazi, Ph.D., and Cynthia L. Ogden, Ph.D., M.R.P, "Attempts to Lose Weight Among Adults in the United States, 2013–2016," CDC, NCHS Data Brief No. 313, July 2018, https://www.cdc.gov/nchs/products/databriefs/db313.htm.

41 John 8:31.

42 Matthew 28:20.

43 Matthew 5:19 and 7:26.

44 John 13:35.

45 See Ephesians 4:32 and Colossians 3:13.

46 John 15:8, NLT.

47 The fruit of the spirit, and their purposes, are listed in Galatians 5:22–25.

48 Luke 14:25–28, NLT.

49 There are several years' worth of research into the worldview of Americans that are helpful to understand what is happening in our country related to worldview. Among the resources describing the research are the books in our annual worldview series. See George Barna, *American Worldview Inventory 2020–2021* (Glendale, AZ: Arizona Christian University Press, 2021); George Barna, *American Worldview Inventory 2021–2022* (Glendale, AZ: Arizona Christian University Press, 2022); and George Barna, *American Worldview Inventory 2022–2023* (Glendale, AZ: Arizona Christian University Press, 2023).

50 For more information based on how people grow spiritually, my exploration of the spiritual journeys of more than 17,000 people is described in George Barna, *Maximum Faith: Live Like Jesus, Experience Genuine Transformation* (Ventura, CA: Metaformation, 2011). One of the core findings from that project was that people grow spiritually primarily through a one-on-one discipling relationship.

51 Barna, *American Worldview Inventory* 2022–2023.

52 Ibid.

CHAPTER 5

53 This information is from the annual worldview survey conducted by the Cultural Research Center at Arizona Christian University. To read about the 2023 statistics, please visit www.Cultural-ResearchCenter.com. These statistics are taken from the report, "Incidence of Biblical Worldview Shows Significant Change Since the Start of the Pandemic," accessible at that website, based on a representative national sample of 2,000 adults.

54 This is based on a survey of adults conducted by the Center for Biblical Worldview, a ministry of the Family Research Council, in 2021 among a nationally representative sample of 1,000 adults. Further information about that survey can be accessed at www.frc.org.

55 Ibid.

56 Romans 7:18b–19.

57 For a plethora of examples, see Frank Viola and George Barna, *Pagan Christianity?* (Carol Stream, IL: Tyndale House Publishers, 2008).

58 While this section describes the seven cornerstones, a more extensive discussion of these factors is contained in a small volume specifically about these foundational principles. See George Barna, *The 7 Cornerstones of a Biblical Worldview* (Glendale, AZ: Arizona Christian University Press, 2023).

59 This information was originally published in the report, "Research Identifies the Best Starting Point for Developing a Biblical Worldview." This report is based upon the annual worldview survey conducted by the Cultural Research Center at Arizona Christian University, based on a representative national sample of 2,000 adults. It is accessible at https://www.arizonachristian.edu/wp-content/uploads/2023/03/CRC-Release-2nd-2023-Final.pdf.

60 Romans 3:23.

61 Mark 12:29–30.

62 John 13:34.

63 James 2:19–20.

64 James 1:22.

65 This teaching appears in Matthew 13, Mark 4, and Luke 8.

66 These factors are operationalized in the personal assessments we conduct with people each year in the *American Worldview Inventory*. If you are interested in seeing how your worldview fares in relation to these criteria, you are invited to take the ACU Worldview Assessment (www.ACUWorldviewAssessment.com), from which you will receive a confidential and personalized report with the results. Those results will be shown in relation to national norms, to provide some analytic context. By June 2024, the Cultural Research Center at ACU expects to have similar, grade-appropriate worldview assessments available online for students in the fourth, eighth, and twelfth grades.

CHAPTER 6

67   Mark 10:13–16; Matthew 21:14–16.

68   For greater detail related to the substance of the seven cornerstones and insights into why those cornerstones matter (i.e., so what?), see George Barna, *The 7 Cornerstones of a Biblical Worldview*.

69   Luke 14:27. Also in Matthew 16:24.

CHAPTER 7

70   Ecclesiastes 11:9; Deuteronomy 29:29; Matthew 12:36; Hebrews 4:13.

71   Hebrews 13:17.

72   Shane Idleman, *Not a Fan: Becoming a Completely Committed Follower of Jesus* (Grand Rapids, MI: Zondervan, 2011).

73   The only worldview I know of that treats behavior and beliefs in a worldview as being of similar importance—based on the notion that behavior is proof of the belief—is the ACU Worldview Assessment. That evaluation tool can be accessed at www.ACUWorldviewAssessment.com.

CHAPTER 8

74   "Landmark Report: U.S. Teens Use an Average of Nine Hours of Media Per Day, Tweens Use Six Hours," Common Sense Media,

Nov. 3, 2015, https://www.commonsensemedia.org/press-releas-es/landmark-report-us-teens-use-an-average-of-nine-hours-of-media-per-day-tweens-use-six-hours

Also reported in "Teens spend more time on media each day than sleeping, study finds," by Matthew Diebel, *USA Today*, 3 Nov. 2015, https://www.usatoday.com/story/news/na-tion/2015/11/03/teens-spend-more-time-media-each-day-than-sleeping-survey-finds/75088256/.

75 Gary W. Small, MD, et al, "Brain Health Consequences of Digital Technology Use," 2020, *Dialogues in clinical neuroscience*, 22(2), 179–187, https://doi.org/10.31887/DCNS.2020.22.2/gsmall.

76 Kalpana Srivastava, et al, "Social media and mental health challenges," 2019, *Industrial Psychiatry Journal*, 28 (2), 155–159. https://doi.org/10.4103/ipj.ipj_154_20.

77 Rosalina Richards, PhD; Rob McGee, PhD; Sheila M. Williams, DSc; David Welch, PhD; Robert J. Hancox, MD; "Adolescent Screen Time and Attachment to Parents and Peers," 2010, *Arch Pediatr Adolesc Med.*, 164(3):258-262. https://jamanetwork.com/journals/jamapediatrics/fullarticle/382905. Lei, L. and Wu, Y, "Adolescents' paternal attachment and Internet use," 2007. *Cyberpsychol Behav* 2007;10 (5) 633- 639. https://pubmed.ncbi.nlm.nih.gov/17927530/+

78 Thomas N. Robinson, et al, "Screen Media Exposure and Obesity in Children and Adolescents," 2017, *Pediatrics*, 140 (Suppl

2), S97–S101. https://doi.org/10.1542/peds.2016-1758K.

79 Wallace Witkowski, "Video games are a bigger industry than movies and North American sports combined, thanks to the pandemic," *MarketWatch*, 2 Jan. 2021, https://www.marketwatch.com/story/videogames-are-a-bigger-industry-than-sports-and-movies-combined-thanks-to-the-pandemic-11608654990..

80 The number of video game users worldwide numbered 2.69 billion in 2020 while the global population reached 7.8 billion. That number has been growing by 5.5% year over year and is expected in 2023 to reach 3 billion video game users out of a global population of 8 billion. See Nestor Gilbert's extensive report on global video game use in "Number of Gamers Worldwide 2022/2023: Demographics, Statistics, and Predictions," *FinancesOnline*, 18 May 2023, https://financesonline.com/number-of-gamers-worldwide/.

81 Mike Snyder, "Two-thirds of Americans, 227 million, play video games. For many games were an escape, stress relief in pandemic," *USA Today*, 13 July 2021, https://www.usatoday.com/story/tech/gaming/2021/07/13/video-games-2021-covid-19-pandemic/7938713002/.

82 "APA Reaffirms Position on Violent Video Games and Violent Behavior," American Academy of Pediatrics, March 3, 2020, https://www.apa.org/news/press/releases/2020/03/violent-video-games-behavior. "Virtual Violence," American Academy of

Pediatrics, Policy Statement, 01 Aug. 2016, https://publications. aap.org/pediatrics/article/138/2/e20161298/52469/Virtual-Violence. "Violent Video Games and Young People," Harvard Health Publishing, Harvard Medical School, October 1, 2010, https://www.health.harvard.edu/newsletter_article/violent-video-games-and-young-people.#:~:text=The%20view%20endorsed%20by%20organizations,harm%20children%20in%20 other%20ways.

83 Considerable research has been published suggesting positive effects of video games on the brain. This article summarizes much of that research: Denilson T. Brilliant, Rui Nouchi, and Ryuta Kawashima, "Does Video Gaming Have Impacts on the Brain: Evidence from a Systematic Review," 2019, *Brain Sciences*, *9*(10), 251, https://doi.org/10.3390/brainsci9100251. This article also offers a fairly comprehensive overview of research into these positive effects: Steven Dekker and Christ Slotboom, "Benefits of recreational gaming," 2023, *International Journal of Esports*, https://www.ijesports.org/article/96/html.

CHAPTER 9

84 These statistics are based on the *American Worldview Inventory 2023*, a nationwide, representative sampling of 2,000 adults, conducted by the Cultural Research Center at Arizona Christian University. The survey, the fourth in an annual series of

worldview evaluations of Americans, was completed in January 2023. The survey included a subgroup of 650 born-again Christians eighteen or older, determined on natural incidence, based upon their claim to be certain that they will experience eternal life in Heaven solely because they have confessed their sins and accepted Jesus Christ as their Savior.

85 These statistics are from a national survey of 1,000 pastors of Christian churches conducted by the Cultural Research Center at Arizona Christian University in February and March 2022. To read more about this survey, consult the reports accessible at www. CulturalResearchCenter.com. Those reports include "Shocking Results Concerning the Worldview of Christian Pastors," published May 10, 2022.

86 Digest of Educational Statistics, U.S. Department of Education, National Center for Education Statistics, 2022, https://nces. ed.gov/programs/digest/2022menu_tables.asp.

87 These conclusions are based upon data drawn from surveys among parents conducted by the American Culture and Faith Institute in 2017 and 2018. The most insightful of those surveys regarding parenting and the role of education were FullView™ 17–3 and FullView™ 18–4, each conducted among a national sample of 1,000 adults.

CHAPTER 10

88 2 Corinthians 10:3-5.

89 Romans 12:2.

90 James 5:16.

91 Romans 8:27-30.

BIBLIOGRAPHY

Adrian, William, et al. *Engaging Our World: Christian Worldview from the Ivory Tower to Global Impact.* Tulsa, OK: W & S Academic Press, 2009.

Anderson, Keith R., and Randy D. Reese. *Spiritual Mentoring: A Guide for Seeking and Giving Direction.* Downers Grove, IL: InterVarsity Press, 1999.

Anthony, Michael J. *Introducing Christian Education: Foundations for the Twenty-First Century.* Grand Rapids, MI: Baker Academic, 2006.

Anthony, Michelle. *Spiritual Parenting.* Colorado Springs, CO: David C. Cook, 2010.

Arn, Win and Charles Arn. *The Master's Plan for Making Disciples.* Grand Rapids, MI: Baker Books, 1998.

Astley, Jeff, et al. *Theological Perspectives on Christian Formation: A Reader on Theology and Christian Education.* Grand Rapids, MI: Gracewing, 1996.

Barna, George. *American Worldview Inventory 2020–2021.* Glendale, AZ: Arizona Christian University Press, 2021.

Barna, George. *American Worldview Inventory 2021–2022.* Glendale, AZ: Arizona Christian University Press, 2022.

Barna, George. *American Worldview Inventory 2022–2023.* Glendale, AZ: Arizona Christian University Press, 2023.

Barna, George. *Maximum Faith: Live Like Jesus, Experience Genuine Transformation.* Ventura, CA: Metaformation, 2011.

Barna, George. *Revolutionary Parenting.* Carol Stream, IL: Tyndale House Publishers, 2007.

Barna, George. *The Index of Leading Spiritual Indicators.* Dallas, TX: Word Publishing, 1996.

Barna, George. *Transforming Children into Spiritual Champions.* Grand Rapids, MI: Baker Books, 2003.

Baucham, Voddie T. *Family Driven Faith: Doing What It Takes to Raise Sons and Daughters Who Walk with God.* Wheaton, IL: Crossway Books, 2007.

Berk, Laura. *Child Development.* 7th ed. Boston: Allyn and Bacon, 2006.

Bonhoeffer, Dietrich. *The Cost of Discipleship. Nachfolge.* New York, NY: Touchstone, 1995.

Chatmon, Terence. *Do Your Children Believe? Becoming Intentional About Your Family's Faith and Spiritual Legacy.* Nashville, TN: W Publishing Group, 2017.

Coleman, Robert. *The Master Plan of Discipleship.* Old Tappan, NJ: Fleming Revell Publishing, 1987.

Coles, Robert. *The Moral Intelligence of Children*. New York, NY: Plume Printing, 1998.

Coles, Robert. *The Spiritual Life of Children*. Boston, MA: Houghton Mifflin Company, 1990.

Colson, Charles, and Nancy Pearcey. *How Now Shall We Live?* Carol Stream, IL: Tyndale House, 1999.

Dockery, David S., and Trevin Wax. *Christian Worldview Handbook*. Nashville, TN: Holman Reference, 2019.

Eims, Leroy. *The Lost Art of Disciple Making*. Colorado Springs, CO: Zondervan/NavPress, 1978.

Essa, Eva L. *Introduction to Early Childhood Education. 5th ed*. Delmar, NY: Thomson Delmar Learning, 2007.

Geisler, Norman L., et al. *To Everyone an Answer: A Case for the Christian Worldview: Essays in Honor of Norman L. Geisler*. Downers Grove, IL: InterVarsity Press, 2004.

Henderson, D. Michael. *John Wesley's Class Meeting: A Model for Making Disciples*. Nappanee, IN: Evangel Publishing House, 1997.

Henrichsen, Walter. *Disciples are Made not Born*. Colorado Springs, CO: Cook Communications, 1988.

Holmen, Mark, and Brian Siewert. *Faith@Home Revealed: An Inside Look at Churchgoing Parents*. Crosslake, MN: Faith@Home Press, 2018.

Holt, John Caldwell. *How Children Learn*. New York: Addison-Wesley Publishing Company, 1997.

Horton, Michael Scott. *We Believe: Recovering the Essentials of the Apostles' Creed*. Nashville, TN: Word Publishing, 1998.

Howse, Brannon. *Christian Worldview for Children: Training the Heart and Mind of a Child to Follow Christ*. Collierville, TN: Worldview Weekend Publishing, 2006.

Hull, Bill. *Jesus Christ, Disciplemaker*. Grand Rapids, MI: Baker Books, 2004.

Leman, Kevin, et al. *The Family Matters Handbook*. Nashville, TN: Thomas Nelson Publishers, 1994.

Lewis, C. S. *Mere Christianity*. New York, NY: HarperCollins Publishers, 2009.

Meyer, Joyce. *Battlefield of the Mind: Winning The Battle in Your Mind*. New York, NY: FaithWords, 2011.

Moore, Ralph. *Making Disciples*. Ventura, CA: Regal Books, 2012.

Morrison, George S. *Early Childhood Education Today*. Upper Saddle River, NJ: Merrill/Pearson, 2009.

Mouw, Richard J. *The Challenges of Cultural Discipleship: Essays in the Line of Abraham Kuyper*. Grand Rapids, MI: Wm. B. Eerdmans Publishing Co., 2012.

Myers, Jeff. *Truth Changes Everything: How People of Faith Can Transform the World in Times of Crisis*. Grand Rapids, MI: Baker Books, 2022.

Myers, Jeff. *Understanding the Faith: A Survey of Christian Apologetics*. Manitou Springs, CO: Summit Ministries, 2016.

Phillips, W. Gary, et al. *Making Sense of Your World: A Biblical World View*. Salem, WI: Sheffield Publishing Co., 2008.

Ramsey, Coart and Bryan Smith. *What Is Truth: Evaluating Competing Worldviews*. Greenville, SC: BJU Press, 2010.

Schaeffer, Francis A. *A Christian Manifesto*. Wheaton, IL: Crossway Books, 1984.

Schaeffer, Francis A. *How Should We Then Live? The Rise and Decline of Western Thought and Culture*. Old Tappan, NJ: Fleming H. Revell Co., 1976.

Sire, James W. *The Universe next Door: A Basic Worldview Catalog*. Downers Grove, IL: InterVarsity Press, 2009.

Smith, Christian and Amy Adamczyk. *Handing Down the Faith: How Parents Pass Their Religion on to the Next Generation*. New York, NY: Oxford University Press, 2021.

Smith, Christian, and Melinda Lundquist Denton. *Soul Searching: The Religious and Spiritual Lives of American Teenagers*. New York, NY: Oxford University Press, 2005.

Sproul, R. C. *Essential Truths of the Christian Faith*. Wheaton, IL: Tyndale House, 1992.

Stephen, Alain. *Why We Think the Things We Think: Philosophy in a Nutshell*. London: Michael O'Mara Books Limited, 2017.

Stott, John R. W. *Basic Christianity*. Downers Grove, IL: IVP Books, 2008.

Sunshine, Glenn S. *Why You Think the Way You Do: The Story of Western Worldviews from Rome to Home*. Grand Rapids, MI: Zondervan, 2009.

Viola, Frank and George Barna. *Pagan Christianity?* Carol Stream, IL: Tyndale House Publishers, 2008.

Wright, N. T. *Following Jesus*. Grand Rapids, MI: William Eerdmans Publishing, 1994.

Zacharias, Ravi K. *Beyond Opinion: Living the Faith That We Defend.* Nashville, TN: Thomas Nelson, 2008.

Zimmerman, Carle C. *Family and Civilization.* Wilmington, DE: ISI Books, 2008.

ACKNOWLEDGMENTS

A volume such as this is a cumulative work, developed over the course of decades and built upon dozens of surveys and interactions. Trying to identify all the people whose input and influence have impacted the end product is a fruitless task. I will list some of those whose contribution is undeniable, but I apologize to those whose name is not listed yet whose added value is one of the many building blocks embedded within the contours of this resource.

Many people at Arizona Christian University, including students, faculty, and staff, have helped make this book a reality. Dr. Tracy Munsil, Publisher of Arizona Christian University Press and Executive Director of the Cultural Research Center, has been part of the heartbeat of this book. Her continual support for the struggle of getting the research funded and completed, managing a variety of interns, and then producing a book from two years of toil on this project has been unwavering and irreplaceable.

The book contains contributions from of a number of ACU students who interned with the Cultural Research Center and participated in various aspects of the research development and implementation. Their energy and commitment have added great value. Our interns assisted with content analyses of specified media vehicles, preliminary manuscript editing, interviewing of key subjects, and developing secondary analyses. My thanks go to Rachel Anklam van den Berg, Russell Bivens, Sarah Crank Mancuso, Caleb Doerksen, Abigayle Fesmire, Annabelle Camoirano Furr, Haile Gleason, Caelan Merryman, Lyrah Panarigan, Savannah Smith, and Macy Spengler.

Dr. Adam Rasmussen, CRC Fellow, and an ACU professor, freed up my time by taking on some of the media interviews that were scheduled for me during the month while I wrote the book. His expertise in worldview has proven invaluable in multiple ways.

Monica Lievsay served as a Research Fellow at CRC for six months and helped develop the research among children's ministries, developed some of the content analysis procedures and trained interns to conduct those analyses, and collected secondary data used to help shape the entire project.

Generous support for the publication of this book also came from Lynn and Robert Torcolini.

My friends and colleagues at the Family Research Council have been invaluable partners in making this book and related resources a reality. In particular I am grateful to work with spiritual warriors such as Tony Perkins, Brent Keilen, Harold Harper, and David Closson.

A group of experts on ministry to young people were invaluable in assisting us in developing the research among effective children's ministries. My thanks go to Sean Sweet of the Four-Five-Six ministry to adolescents, Jim Burns of Home Word, Matt Markins of Awana, and Mark DeVries of Ministry Architects for pointing us to the right practitioners. Further gratitude is expressed to Hannah Bush, Chip Henderson, Randy Isola, Sam Luce, Reggie Rice, McKenna Shrum, Kris Smoll, and Heidi Winter for sharing their insights into church-based ministry to children and parents.

The research would not have been completed without the tireless and strategic efforts of my longtime research partners at Braun Research. Special thanks go to the team members I work with most closely, including Paul Braun, Dave Oshman, Jay Schleisman, and the late Shayne Poole.

Connecting us with the media regarding this project has been a long-term project that has been capably handled by Jason Jones and Mark Breta of Jones Literary.

Publishing the book would not have happened without the wise and skilled guidance of Esther Fedorkevich and her team at The Fedd Agency.

My grandson, JD Barron, helped in the development of the Seven Cornerstones research.

My wife, Nancy, once again surrendered me to a book project, taking on multiple responsibilities in my absence.

ABOUT THE AUTHOR

George Barna is a professor at Arizona Christian University and Director of Research at the Cultural Research Center at Arizona Christian University, focusing on worldview assessment and development, and cultural transformation. He is also the Senior Research Fellow at Family Research Council's Center for Biblical Worldview and a Fellow at the Townsend Institute at Concordia University.

He was the founder of The Barna Group (which he sold in 2009), the Barna Institute, the American Culture and Faith Institute, and Metaformation. Through these entities, he has conducted groundbreaking research on worldview, cultural transformation, ministry applications, spiritual development, and politics.

He has provided research and strategy for several hundred parachurch ministries, thousands of Christian churches, the U.S. military, and Fortune 500 companies. Having begun his research career in the political arena, he has provided polling for numerous political campaigns and has provided polling and strategy to four presidential candidates. He has also served on multiple boards of directors and advisory boards.

Raising Spiritual Champions is the sixtieth book that Barna has authored or co-authored. His books have addressed social and religious trends, worldview, leadership, spiritual development, church dynamics, and cultural transformation. They include *New York Times* and *Amazon* bestsellers and several award-winning books. His books have been translated into more than a dozen foreign languages. He is a frequent speaker at events throughout the world, having spoken at more than a thousand events during the course of his career, including events in fourteen different countries.

Prior to joining the faculty of ACU, Barna taught at several universities and seminaries, served as the teaching pastor of a large, multi-ethnic church, pastored a house church, and helped to start several churches. He has also served as an elder in several congregations.

After graduating summa cum laude from Boston College, Barna earned two master's degrees from Rutgers University and received a doctorate from Dallas Baptist University.

Barna and his wife, Nancy, attended high school, college, and graduate school together before marrying in the Princeton University Chapel in 1978. They have three adopted daughters and three grandchildren and currently live on the central California coast and in the Phoenix area.

When his schedule allows, he enjoys spending time with his grandchildren, relaxing at the beach or on a cruise, watching the NY

Yankees, playing bass guitar and listening to the blues, hanging out with his blind dog, Ray Charles, visiting comedy clubs, or watching comedy specials, and reading novels.

RELATED BOOKS BY GEORGE BARNA

George Barna has written sixty books related to faith and culture. Most of his books are based on research that he has conducted through the various research organizations he has led, starting with the Barna Group (which he sold in 2009) and including three other entities since then: Metaformation Inc., the American Culture and Faith Institute, and the Cultural Research Center at Arizona Christian University.

Based on the studies Barna has completed with those organizations, he has provided cutting-edge insight into the state of the culture and how faith intersects—or does not intersect—with American culture. If you are interested in his research and analyses regarding various aspects of society these days, and the implications of the findings for our future, you might consider these books, available at amazon.com, on the CRC website (culturalresearchcenter.com), or through the website GeorgeBarna.com.

| RELATED BOOKS |

Helping Millennials Thrive: Practical Wisdom for a Generation in Crisis, ACU Press, 2023.

American Worldview Inventory 2022–23, ACU Press, 2023.

American Worldview Inventory 2021–22, ACU Press, 2022.

American Worldview Inventory 2020–21, ACU Press, 2021.

Fearless Parenting (with Jimmy Myers), Baker Books, 2017.

America at the Crossroads, Baker Books, 2016.

U-Turn (with David Barton), Charisma House, 2014.

Maximum Faith, SGG Publishing, 2011.

The Cause within You (with Matthew Barnett), Tyndale House, 2011.

Master Leaders, Tyndale House, 2009.

Pagan Christianity? (with Frank Viola), Tyndale House, 2008.

Revolutionary Parenting, Tyndale House, 2007.

Revolution, Tyndale House, 2005.

Transforming Children into Spiritual Champions, Regal Books, 2003.

Think Like Jesus, Integrity Publishing, 2003.

ABOUT THE CULTURAL RESEARCH CENTER AT ARIZONA CHRISTIAN UNIVERSITY

The Cultural Research Center (CRC) at Arizona Christian University is located on the school's campus in Glendale, Arizona, in the Phoenix metropolitan area. CRC is guided by George Barna, Professor and Director of Research, and Tracy Munsil, Associate Professor and Executive Director.

CRC is a pioneer in worldview research. It began an annual tracking study of the worldview of Americans, the *American Worldview Inventory*, in 2020. That same year, CRC also introduced the *ACU Student Worldview Inventory*, which is administered to every ACU student at the start of each academic year, plus a final administration among students just prior to their graduation. That longitudinal research enables the University to track the worldview development of its student body and to make appropriate changes to the educational process based upon objective data. The Center also provides the *ACU Worldview Assessment*, a worldview evaluation tool used by individuals, schools, and churches. A variety of research-driven books, study guides, and other resources are published in cooperation with Arizona University Press.

The Cultural Research Center also conducts a variety of national research studies to explore the intersection of faith and culture. It shares that information through its partnerships with a growing network of Bible-centric, theologically conservative Christian ministries.

Access to the results of surveys conducted by CRC, as well as additional information about the Cultural Research Center, can be gained at www.CulturalResearchCenter.com. To examine the Statement of Faith that guides the Center, or for more information about Arizona Christian University, please visit www.arizonachristian.edu.

OUR MISSION

Family Research Council's mission is to serve in the kingdom of God by championing faith, family, and freedom in public policy and the culture from a biblical worldview.

FRC.ORG